Customer Value Starvation Can Kill

Customer Value Starvation Can Kill

Prevention and Cure

Gautam Mahajan
Walter Vieira

Foreword by Philip Kotler

iiBEP
BUSINESS EXPERT PRESS
Leader in applied, concise business books

First published in 2021 by
Business Expert Press, LLC
222 East 46th Street, New York, NY 10017
www.businessexpertpress.com

ISBN-13: 978-1-95253-858-2 (paperback)
ISBN-13: 978-1-95253-859-9 (e-book)

Business Expert Press Service Systems and Innovations in Business and Society Collection

Collection ISSN: 2326-2664 (print)
Collection ISSN: 2326-2699 (electronic)

Cover and interior design by S4Carlisle Publishing Services Private Ltd., Chennai, India

First edition: 2021

10 9 8 7 6 5 4 3 2 1

Dedication

This book is dedicated to customers who suffer Customer Value Starvation and often have no recourse. May this book help businesses change this from happening.
And to our Wives, who have suffered us for long years and recently through the Corona Virus lockdown.

Description

Customer Value Starvation is a common disease in companies, both small and large, that is difficult to diagnose. It is a silent killer, like many cancers. By the time it is diagnosed, it is generally late, sometimes, too late.

Mahajan and Vieira have put their expertise together to show how Value Starvation is overlooked by companies. This causes irritation and frustration to customers in their interaction with the company and its personnel—in person, on the telephone, via the website or e-mail.

The book identifies customer DNA (Do Not Annoy) factors and suggests how to minimize complaints and ensure customer loyalty and long-term company profitability and success.

Philip Kotler, the world's marketing guru, has said, "This book will help you think freshly about your business mission and success."

Seven well-known experts on the subject, such as Shep Hyken, have contributed articles to this book.

Read *Customer Value Starvation Can Kill,* and make life easier for your customers and yourself!

Keywords

value; value starvation; value destruction; value deprivation; customer; business; company; customer value starvation; loyalty; profitability; customer value

Praise for *Customer Value Starvation Can Kill*

"This book discusses starvation, and its opposite. After reading this book, you'll be full of ideas, strategies, and tactics to help you deliver more value in the form of customer service and experience."
—**Shep Hyken, Customer Service/Experience Expert and NYT and WSJ Bestselling Author of** *The Amazement Revolution*

"Makes a good read. It has plenty of anecdotes. It can become a bible for customer care people (not that they care for customers) if they take the trouble to read it."
—**P. Jayaram, Visiting Professor at Amrita School of Communication, Coimbatore. Formerly, Head of the Department of Communication and Senior Journalist, India**

"Customer Value Starvation is a very slippery slope. Mahajan and Vieira do an excellent job of showing how easily companies start down the slope without even realizing it, and then how difficult it is to recover customers from the fall. They also give the manager tips on how to avoid the slope in the first place. You cannot read this book without being profoundly changed, with a newfound enthusiasm for customer centricity and value creation. If enough people read this book, the world will be a much improved place."
—**Moshe Davidow, Customer Service Expert, CEO of Service2Profit and Professor at the Ono Academic Center, Israel**

"This is truly a handbook. Brief, simple language, no jargon, with a balance of theory and examples—a VIEIRA hallmark. I had never realized how many minor irritations have been absorbed by me unconsciously, and influenced my attitude towards products and services. This book by Walter Vieira and Gautam Mahajan will really help much of the business community, especially in the B to C area. My best wishes for this significant contribution."
—**Harish Mehta, Co Founder/Past President, NASSCOM, Founder/ Chairman, Onward Technologies, India**

"I have always firmly believed that nothing can ensure consumer loyalty, more than the creation and fervent maintenance of strong bonds between the customer, and the first line and at every level of customer contact…from the company or outsourced "call" operator or the user friendliness of the website to every contact point, including the salesman at the point of sale!

Somehow, this is generally forgotten. Or, neglected.

Top management gets too involved with balance sheets, top lines, and bottom lines. The result? Small customer irritations go unnoticed. The company keeps losing customers, and top management tends to realize this too late. This book is a welcome warning bell—for those who are still prepared to listen."

—**Roger C. B. Pereira, ex-Board Member, International Advertising Association (IAA), New York; Founder, IAA Chapters: Indonesia, Singapore & Sri Lanka and Chairman and Founder India Chapter; and Founder, Advertising Standards Council of India**

Contents

Acknowledgments

Our thanks to Professor Philip Kotler, the world's marketing guru, for bringing the authors together and suggesting we write this book, and for his generous endorsement.

We appreciate very much the Observations on the book written by Winn Knight.

A special thanks to Larry Malarkar for his useful comments on the book, to make it better.

Our thanks also to the following experts and contributors to the art and science of Customer Value Starvation, who have shared their thoughts and views through their contribution to this book.

- *Marc Grainer, Chair; Scott M. Broetzmann, President & CEO; David Beinhacker, Chief Research Officer all of Customer Care Measurement & Consulting, USA*
- *Paul Selby, Product Marketing Director for ServiceNow, USA*
- *Shep Hyken, Customer Service Expert, USA*
- *V. N. Bhattacharya, Adjunct Professor, IIM Bangalore, and Independent Consultant Business & Corporate Strategy, India*
- *B. S. Nagesh, Chairman of Retailers Association of India; Founder, TRRAIN; Nonexecutive Chairman, Shoppers Stop Ltd., India*
- *Denyse Drummond-Dunn, President & Chief Catalyst of C3Centricity, Switzerland*
- *Moshe Davidow, Customer Service Expert, CEO of Service2Profit and Professor at the Ono Academic Center, Israel*

Foreword

by Philip Kotler

I am delighted to read the fresh ideas in this book about Value Creation, Value Destruction, Value Deprivation, and Value Starvation. Companies tend to think that repeat purchases and customer satisfaction are sufficient indicators that the company is serving the customer well. Yet, all this time, the customer may be deprived or starved of value.

My two longtime friends, Walter Vieira and Gautam Mahajan, both eminent marketers, got together and discussed their ideas with top managers and thinkers and asked for their reflections on how to prevent and manage Customer Value Starvation. This is the silent and insidious killer of companies. Companies do not realize the presence of this disease in the company unless it is late, or sometimes, too late.

This book will help you think freshly about your business mission and success. Customers and other stakeholders deserve more than you have been giving them. It is not a matter of spending more money.

The environment is constantly changing and therefore there are opportunities all the time to upgrade the product and service, rather than sitting back and resting on laurels of the past. It is a matter of thinking more deeply, creatively, and continuously about how to create and deliver value to your stakeholders.

Philip Kotler is undoubtedly the most famous marketing guru in the world. His book *Marketing Management* has been around for about 50 years and is now in its 15th edition.

Introduction

Why This Book in 2021: *Customer Value Starvation Can KILL*

How do you keep happy customers when cutting costs is essential? (Airline costs are going up, fares are going down. Where is the money going to come from?) Singapore Airlines is a customer service leader and lower in costs than similar airlines. Ten customer leaders in different fields have the lowest costs—because they have happy customers.

We need to avoid complaints (go toward zero complaints or at least zero Customer Value Starvation complaints) and get contented customers by not starving them of satisfaction. Starvation causes complaints, and costs the company time, money, and effort to rectify them. Why not just work toward getting rid of this source of annoyance. Learn "Do Not Annoy" the Customer!

Customer Value Starvation increases customer and company effort, makes them do more work.

We are all so happy when companies regularly provide Customer Value Creation. We also are not pleased with companies that, in an obvious fashion, indulge in Customer Value Destruction and Customer Value Deprivation (defined and discussed in this book).

Customer Value Starvation is a more benign and often unnoticed form of Value Destruction. It is a niggling, seemingly unimportant issue that causes customers short-term pain and is therefore unnoticed by the company, but reduces the value to the customer. For example, giving you a wrong address to write to and your letter comes back (or worse still you visit a nonexistent location because the company did not update the address on its information page or website).

Customer Value Starvation happens when you irritate a customer or are unhelpful to him. Or when there is no follow-up. Or when you have ridiculous and rigid rules.

From Shep Hyken's article: Don't Let Your Customers Fall In The Expected Experiences Gap, with permission(See Shep Hyken's article "The Incomplete Answer," https://hyken.com/customer-service-training/the-incomplete-answer/).

The aim of companies should not only be avoiding Customer Value Starvation (although this is a necessary first step) but increasing Customer Value.

This book is about Value Starvation and how you can kill customers and your company. Value Starvation is what happens when you deny a customer very basic needs in doing business with you. Often, this is done unwittingly or because the company is too busy trying to improve profits or experience.

The mantra to prevent Customer Value Starvation is do not annoy (DNA). Understand the Customer's DNA factors!

Value Starvation occurs when a company posts a link on its website that does not work or fails to update a product spec or does not allow you access to the right person for your solution or the customer cannot get through to your telephone or gets no response to an e-mail or an incomplete answer.

An example is an airline changing a flight timing and failing to inform you.

Value Destruction happens when knowingly or unknowingly companies destroy value. Examples:

When the airline sends your bags to the wrong destination or a hotel denies you a prepaid hotel room.

Note the line between Value Starvation and Value Destruction is often blurred and depends on the customer's perception.

Companies that starve customers of value consistently end up destroying value and can die. Most companies are killed over a longer period of time, by a cancer that does not show major symptoms, but finally ends in death, because companies wake up too late or not at all. That is Customer Value Starvation. Instead of Value Creation there is Value Dilution. Let us give you some examples of businesses in India, that have died or are dying:

> Tata Sky is heralded by the Tata group as an example of great service. It probably has the worst systems. You cannot get a proper answer on how much you owe, or even reach them on landlines, using their help button on screen. These numbers do not work. They also say for toll free calls go to the website, making the customer do the work. I could not get through to the number. It also gives a number to give a missed call to. It does not work! Channel 613 to which I was subscribed, was not working. The online message on the TV screen said contact Tata Sky by text message. I asked them to restore channel 613 via a text message. The response was, it is working. I am unable to get through to Tata Sky to tell them it is NOT.
>
> Clearly a case of Customer Value Starvation!

The yellow cabs (Delhi taxi service) are dying because of continuous value starvation. They do not give you point-to-point service, they do not adhere to the meter, they insist on being hired for a minimum of 4 hours, or when you want to go from Point A to B, they want you to pay the return fare. Competing services such as Uber and Ola are destroying the old-fashioned customer-starving taxi services.

Take landlines, particularly MTNL, India's public sector telephone company, who at one time were a monopoly. They starved customers of value: poor service, poor response, not caring. Recently, a friend locked down due to the Covid-19 crisis complained he could not do anything because MTNL had not fixed his broadband in 6 weeks. Can you imagine such value starvation that will lead to death (of the company) especially at times that the Internet is absolutely necessary?

There are streets in Chennai that I visited many years ago that had two light poles almost adjacent to each other. The old ones (3 years old) were rusting and falling down. Some company had sold poles based on price that could not meet specifications (and probably lined some pockets)—a clear case of value starvation leading to death of the poles and the company.

That is why this book focuses on Customer Value Starvation, since it can kill companies. Continued Value Starvation leads to value destruction and death.

For most people today when they get so involved with technology and the progress the world has made in the last 50 years, there is a great danger of losing perspective and the view of the broad picture of a business and what it is meant to be.

Companies are so concerned with Customer Value Creation (and that is a good thing) that they sometimes forget that in the whole process we may also be involved with exactly the opposite, and concurrently!

With all the technology available to us today, we may end up building a beautiful castle, but built on a foundation of sand.

Customer Value Starvation Can Kill is a guideline for managers in large companies and small, to ensure that their companies are on a solid foundation, and they then keep building on this, because they have laid the foundation for many more floors than earlier anticipated.

Customer Value Starvation Can Kill might seem to be an account of the obvious. But a look at at, for example, Indian buildings, roads, pavements, parks, railways, banking systems, insurance procedures, consumer products, airlines services, telecommunications, and many other areas will convince you why a solid foundation is necessary. Examples are from many countries.

This short book is a plea to businesses to build a solid foundation of customer connection with training at the first point of customer contact to ensure customer loyalty and ensure that companies and customers grow together for mutual benefit and the benefit of the community.

In this long journey, there will certainly be hiccups. They have to be managed. Successful long-term companies have managed them. "What man has done, man can do" is the old adage. And still true.

Even if we succeed in preventing 25 percent of companies—small or large—from starving customers, wittingly or unwittingly, *Customer Value Starvation Can Kill* would have achieved its goal. *Customer Value Starvation Can Kill* is a new offering for those that are start-ups in business and mostly focused on technology improvement. They lack *customer focus* and therefore 40 percent of start-ups fail in just the first few years.

Customer Value Starvation Can Kill is also for those who have been very successful in business or in government, or even in the NGO sector—those who become complacent and more inward looking as a result of such success.

Customer Value Starvation Can Kill is therefore a *back to basics* book, written in a manner that will be appealing to all levels of management, including top management. Again, Customer Value Starvation makes us heed that wise counsel from Philip Kotler: "The more successful a company becomes, the faster it forgets the very lessons that made it successful."

Customer Value Starvation Can Kill (like the book *Who Moved My Cheese*) helps to bring the derailed back on track so that those who manage business, any business, can move forward and continue to make progress to serve all stakeholders.

The book has therefore been kept short and simple, has many real-life examples, and has contributions from some of the experts in management from different countries. This mix makes the book an easy and enjoyable read, as it remains instructive without being didactic. A hallmark of Walter Vieira's 14 other books!!

We are fortunate to share seven articles by experts Marc Grainer, Scott M. Broetzmann, David Beinhacker, Paul Selby, Shep Hyken, V. N. Bhattacharya, B. S. Nagesh, Denyse Drummond-Dunn, and Moshe Davidow. We thank them for their generosity.

There are many examples of Customer Value Starvation given in the book based on real-life situations with various companies/businesses. And

Customer Value Creation also exists in the same companies, in different situations and/or in different geographies. By the same token, Customer Value Starvation does not exist in many other companies.

The examples given are just that: examples. They are not a *criticism* or a *labelling*. These stories are related here so readers can learn from real-life situations.

If you have any experience as customers you would like to share with us, please do send them to us. This will be most welcome.

What Is Value?

Value is a most misunderstood and misused word. As it becomes fashionable to *create value*, more companies are rushing toward the *creating value* mantra. In doing so, they forget Value Starvation and Value Destruction.

It is germane to start this book with a definition of value:

Value Creation is executing proactive, conscious, inspired, or imaginative and even normal actions that increase the overall good and well-being, and the worth of ideas, goods, services, people, or institutions, including society, and all stakeholders (like employees, customers, partners, shareholders, and society), and value waiting to happen.

Value Starvation diminishes the well-being of people and companies. Companies pursue their goal of increasing shareholder wealth. In the process, they fall into the pothole of Customer Value Starvation.

This book shows you how to recognize Value Starvation, how to avoid it, and how to prevent it. This will make you and your companies more effective, more customer centric, and more successful. Preventing Customer Value Starvation reduces your costs, increases customer loyalty and profits.

Remember what Jack Welch, former CEO of GE, said, "If you are not thinking customer, you are not thinking."

Preface

Gautam states: Philip Kotler was talking to me about my book *Value Dominant Logic*. He said I needed to write a lighter book with a message with Walter Vieira, who he called India's greatest marketer. Walter Vieira has been described by Philip Kotler as one of "the best speakers on Marketing in Asia, and perhaps worldwide."

Walter and I had met earlier, and we reconnected to write the book *Customer Value Starvation*. In extreme cases, Value Starvation can lead to Value Destruction. It is up to the reader to decide how bad the Starvation is in the examples in this book. The lack of value availability leads to Value Deprivation.

I have been writing about Value Creation and Destruction, and how focusing on possible Value Destruction can lead to greater Value Creation. Value Starvation is a more unconscious and milder version of Value Destruction. Many companies do not notice it, nor do they try to remove such irritants and become more customer friendly.

> "Yes, we do have a customer-centric movement going on—among customers … (they) are acting more empowered and emboldened and are continually upping their expectations of companies. More than just a 'movement' this is a large rock rumbling downhill at increasing speed that imperils anything in its way."
>
> Marsh, C., P. Sparrow, and M. Hird. 2010. *Is Customer Centricity a Movement or Myth?*

Customers are becoming more aware and demanding and are taking the driver's seat in the company–customer relationship. Overall loyalty has reduced to 8 percent according to a recent Global Millennial Survey.

Here is a book to make you more aware and to become value creators who show they can be truly customer friendly and customer focused as well.

Phil Kotler made the purpose of marketing to create value as shown in the Preface to the latest edition of his book *Marketing Management*

Preface

The Fourteenth Edition of *Principles of Marketing*! Still Creating More Value for You!

The goal of every marketer is to create more value for customers. So it makes sense that our goal for the fourteenth edition is to continue creating more value for you—*our* customer. Our goal is to introduce new marketing students to the fascinating world of modern marketing in an innovative and comprehensive yet practical and enjoyable way. We've poured over every page, table, figure, fact, and example in an effort to make this the best text from which to learn about and teach marketing. Enhanced by mymarketinglab, our online homework and personalized study tool, the fourteenth edition creates exceptional value for both students and professors.

Marketing: Creating Customer Value and Relationships

Top marketers at outstanding companies share a common goal: putting the consumer at the heart of marketing. Today's marketing is all about creating customer value and building profitable customer relationships. It starts with understanding consumer needs and wants, determining which target markets the organization can serve best, and developing a compelling value proposition by which the organization can attract and grow valued consumers. If the organization does these things well, it will reap the rewards in terms of market share, profits, and customer equity.

Five Major Value Themes

From beginning to end, the fourteenth edition of *Principles of Marketing* develops an innovative customer-value and customer-relationships framework that captures the essence of today's marketing. It builds on five major value themes:

1. *Creating value for customers in order to capture value from customers in return.* Today's marketers must be good at *creating value* and *managing customer relationships.* Outstanding marketing companies understand the marketplace and customer needs, design value-creating marketing strategies, develop integrated marketing programs that deliver customer value and delight, and build strong customer relationships. In return, they capture value from customers in the form of sales, profits, and customer loyalty.

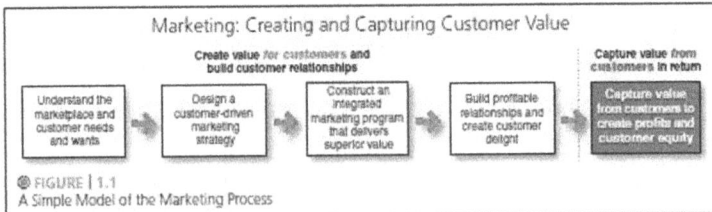

Marketing: Creating and Capturing Customer Value

Create value for customers and build customer relationships				Capture value from customers in return
Understand the marketplace and customer needs and wants	Design a customer-driven marketing strategy	Construct an integrated marketing program that delivers superior value	Build profitable relationships and create customer delight	Capture value from customers to create profits and customer equity

● FIGURE | 1.1
A Simple Model of the Marketing Process

The American Marketing Association released a new definition of marketing: "Marketing is the activity, set of institutions, and processes for creating, communicating, delivering, and exchanging offerings that have value for customers, clients, partners, and society at large."

Thus, in today's marketing, the purpose of a company is all about creating value, as stated by Kotler. Value Starvation negates all these positive thoughts.

Walter adds: I was brought up to think positively. My parents made sure every time I criticized a person, product, or service, they would point out to the positives in the situation and also point out that the negatives were far outweighed by the positives. Looking back now, I realize that it was a good way to bring up children—so they grow up optimists instead of pessimists and this helps to bring a glow to their own lives.

We were also taught to thank the good Lord, our Maker, for the blessings that we have received and perhaps many others would not have been so lucky.

Over the years, I have looked around and seen how progress has been made, by many individuals, and also groups of individuals, who have added value to products and services. They have made them better and better, and we are enjoying the benefits of this all the time. The concept of Value Creation, and of Value Addition, is to help make this a better world. I see the benefits right now in toilets I sometimes need to use—where I do not pull the flush anymore (it's automatic, when you finish using it); where you just put your hands below the tap and the water flows and put your hand under the soap dispenser and the soap flows in limited quantities; where you put your hands under the drier and in a few minutes you emerge from the *washroom* having touched nothing except the door handle, to enter and to exit (there could have been an automatic door). No wonder there are so many books on Customer Value Creation—my co-author here, Gautam Mahajan, has written at least six of them. And that is all to the good. It is positive thinking—a movement to keep making this a better world.

Against this backdrop, we forget that there is also Customer Value Starvation and it is not as rare as many people believe. It is just that customers have become used to careless treatment; they have found that nothing happens even if they complain, and it is better to let things be and go on with the business of living. However, the levels of Customer Value Starvation are so high, if a proper survey is done, that we will make a mistake to just let it be. We need to deal with this issue with as much seriousness as Customer Value Creation. We can considerably increase Customer Value Creation if we create awareness and *reduce* Customer Value Starvation.

Galbraith describes customer centricity as a fundamental paradigm shift—away from the bias of the organization and its agents to operate on the side of the seller (i.e., itself) in any transaction and toward operating "outside-in"—on meeting the needs of the users or purchasers of products or services. This approach to organizing people and work embeds many HR and OD best practices—including self-management, direct and frank communication, individual change agency, and team-based decision-making—and places these qualities firmly in service of better outcomes for the end user, for the business, and for employee engagement.

Galbraith, J. R. 2005. *Designing the Customer-Centric Organization: A Guide to Strategy, Structure, and Process*. New York: Wiley.

It was last year that I had been invited to Goa to give a lecture at a national conference of some industry, and I was to go from Mumbai by the early morning flight and return by the evening flight the same day. I had booked a taxi to take me to the airport at 5 a.m. There was no sign of the taxi till 5.30 am. I tried to get them on the telephone, but they would not pick up the phone. So, I got into my own car and drove fast to the airport. The parking area was far from the airport, so I just parked the car on the roadside outside the Airport Building and rushed in. I was the last passenger to check in, thanks to the kind counter staff, who could have easily said "too late" (value creation here!).

The day went through without a hitch, and I left the hotel at 5 p.m. for the Goa airport. My hosts and the hotel staff helped me to put my bag in the boot of the car, and I was thinking about the problems I would have in Mumbai, with the risk I had taken to just leave the car on the roadside.

After I had checked in and was waiting for the flight, I got a call from the hotel that my bag had been mixed up with the bag of another visitor who had an identical design of bag. My bag was being sent to the airport, posthaste, and could I please retrieve the bag I had checked in and give it to the driver who would be there in half an hour. We went through the whole process, because fortunately there was enough time before the plane took off. And, I landed in Mumbai, to find that my car was not where I had parked it. I had to go to the police to get a clearance, because they had spent an hour in the morning to check whether this car was loaded with bombs, directed at the airport. It is a long story of how I finally got it released, and drove home!

There were just two minor lapses. They were Customer Value Starvation. But they created havoc through my day of travel. Both were easily avoidable. The first with more discipline. The company should ensure drivers wake up in time to do the assignment (as an example, the cab in Mumbai). The second, being careless, in not checking the room number details (I should have checked this also and not taken it for granted) before confidently loading the bag into the car.

Both showed deficiency in service. This is Customer Value Starvation, which will end in Value Destruction.

The more I looked around, the more I felt that there is a crying need for individuals and companies to be aware whether they are involving themselves in Customer Value Starvation, without being conscious of this. The purpose of this book is to create such awareness and thereby improve our service to the customer. This will make the effort to create Customer Value much more effective, than concentrating only on Customer Value Creation.

And implementing programs to prevent Customer Value Starvation as well as Customer Value Destruction will also be far more economical programs for Customer Value Creation. This will strengthen overall efforts at improving Customer Value.

We could have given many more examples, and also from many more industries. However, we have kept the book brief, anecdotal, easy to read—enough to make one realize that the answer lies at that final point of customer contact supported by the back end. Unfortunately, this point is far removed from the power centers at the top of the company. Unless they occasionally step out and meet some of the crowd that helps the company make profits, such a change will not come about.

This book examines Customer Centricity and Customer Value Starvation, in a folksy, anecdotal fashion and explains why in spite of what all business leaders know, they still do not get it.

They forget they too are customers. Perhaps, they should take a day a month where they are true customers of railways or banks or any private sector company and see how they are treated.

- Many of them are doing things that do not impact customers in the right way, or
- They do not feel it is necessary to make customers happy...*what should they do?* or
- They just do not notice what is happening. or
- Worse, they do not care.

The book brings the real world to their notice. It suggests what they should do.

- CEOs and executives should become more aware of what is happening.
- They need to bring awareness to customers that they are not alone.
- They need to suggest a way of improving: avoid Value Starvation and progress toward Customer Loyalty.

When people enter their offices, they don the executive hat. They take off their customer hat. This book will show how the customer hat and the executive hat can combine so that we all avoid Customer Value Starvation.

It is the principle of what Professor Kotler calls "Working toward the common good."

This book therefore is also an appeal to top management to remember Peter Drucker's maxim: "The only reason for the existence of the company is to create and keep a customer."

Observations on Customer Value Starvation

by Winn Knight

Value Is a Currency

As a company, you have a profit and loss account with each of your customers. You invest money in them to build brand awareness, relationships, and loyalty and get them to buy your products and services—at a profit.

Your customers, on the other hand, invest their time, emotions, experiences, and hard cash in you to obtain that product or service that will satisfy their needs, wants, and aspirations.

You both bring value to this transaction. It is inclusive and is built on the two essential characteristics of trust and commitment. And by delivering superior value, you will reap an equitable return on your investment.

I am honored and delighted to find myself among these two eminent writers in marketing, to add a word...or two to Gautam Mahajan and Walter Vieira's thought-provoking and practical book *Customer Value Starvation Can Kill.*

Customer Value Starvation leads to a slow death. Its pace is different for different companies and often not recognized until historical data and figures show the decline. The authors' book, filled with practical examples and great insights into the real world, is a valuable reference during this unsettling period that is witnessing the demise of many companies—large and small.

You will recognize many examples in their book that will resonate with your own personal circumstances.

Value Drives Customer Profitability

Customers are the foundation of your business, and your values are the pillars that sustain and grow value for your stakeholders across the ever-evolving Customer Economy, also known as the Me Economy.

The important thing to remember is that *people are people,* irrespective of whether they are our employees, customers, society and shareholders or our friends and family. Their *changing* outlook on life has an impact on how we do business, how we build relationships, grow loyalty, and achieve profitability—and how we bring value to their daily lives.

Customers are not interested in how we deliver the value we promise them, what, when, where, or why, as long as they get what they want from us (or perceive that they get it), when they want it, especially when it comes to customer service, that is, when they are willing to pull out their wallets.

We are so busy managing our companies that we have forgotten our customers. And we are so busy changing the rules that we have forgotten how to play the game.

Radical changes are taking place—old, staid business processes are being reimagined and redesigned with both hard and soft, tangible and intangible values built into the customer journey—activating what is sometimes a completely new support chain of collaborators.

In this Age of Disruption, (or is it now Eternal Disruption), value creation for your stakeholders is the glue, that is, the key reason for you being in business.

Customer Value Starvation Can Kill is a well-written and easy to read book with a refreshing and inspirational outlook and important guidance on how *not to* starve your customers…or your profits.

I wish you well to read and enjoy it.

Winnifred Knight: Marketer at Large, South Africa.

SECTION 1

Understanding Value Terminology

In this book, we often write about value deprivation, value destruction, and value starvation. Sometimes there is an overlap between these terms, and sometimes destruction follows starvation. In the following pages we help you walk through the meanings and how these things happen.

Sometimes the opposite happens. We are positively and happily surprised by a company. We get into the realm of value creation. Our aim in this book is to help convert you from causing value starvation and destruction to creating value.

Winn Knight from South Africa introduced me to the term Value Starvation. In my vocabulary, this is not as bad as value destruction but about half way there. Most of the time when customers are getting starved of value, the company does not even notice.

What causes Value Starvation?

1. The product or service may cause trouble to customers. This may not be obvious to the company executives. It may irritate a customer. It could mildly upset a customer.
2. What is important to the customers may not be important in the view of the executives. Unfortunately, those who notice Customer Value Starvation are mostly customers and can do nothing much to influence the company. Those that can influence the company are executives and employees of a company, but they do not notice or care about Customer Value Starvation.

   The customer often thinks about the end result. The printer is just not a printer, but must connect to the internet and the computer, and should be easy to use and require no time and effort. To the printer company the printer is the main focus, not customer thinking!

3. The convenience of the company may be more important than the convenience of the customer. Or the company rules are rigid. Shep Hyken gives an example of standing in line at a fast-food restaurant. He was next to be served while the lady in front ordered breakfast. When his turn came, he ordered breakfast, and the girl at the counter said no breakfast after 10.30 a.m. It was 10.31 a.m. How rigid can you get? This is *starvation* too. Shep walked to the next restaurant at the mall. The first restaurant lost a customer.

Let's examine someone trying to reach an executive in a company. There may or may not be a phone number or an e-mail address. Let's assume there is an e-mail address such as info@xyz.com. Let's say you want to interview the CEO, and send a message. Perhaps there is no response as the e-mail is checked (if at all checked) by a junior executive.

Bank of America

Try reaching the Bank of America. You can only send a complaint through their site, but only if it matches the drop down menu.

Anything different is not possible.

They say the way to get to someone is to call.

They give a number for those outside the United States to call collect. I was in Ireland when I had a problem. I tried calling collect and was told that this number does not accept collect calls. I finally tried calling direct and would hang up after 20–30 minutes of calling. I eventually got through but my problem was not solved.

This may not be obvious to the CX (customer experience) designer. Or his attitude could be, I am the gatekeeper, and so this message cannot go to the CEO. Or this message is not important, and so he ignores it. This reminds me of an Indian company pavilion at a trade fair, 30 years ago. It was difficult to get into the pavilion, because the indian company did not want to be bothered with seemingly inconsequential people. I entered another pavilion at the same trade fair of a very large company with open access, because a person at the booth asked me to come in.

He turned out to be the CEO. He told me that they wanted people to come in and see what they had. That is why they were displaying at the fair. The reader can easily notice the difference in attitude.

Many companies around the world are saying you cannot contact us; only we can contact you. This is the case of the one-way contact.

Lastly, preventing people reaching your company executives is for the convenience

> Once I complained about a credit card charge. They said they would look into it. A few days later, I realized the charge was genuine. There was no way of letting them know except via calling. I had the same problems of calling from India. I finally gave up.
>
> Three months later, they came to me with many pages of paper proving the charge was genuine. What a waste of time, all due to Customer Value Starvation!

of the company not the convenience of the customer. For example, you force a customer to put all his credentials in a mail (no e-mail address) through the website. Let's assume the customer is told to make a call and, like me, is in India and making a call to the United States (it's difficult with the 12-hour time difference, cost, etc.).

Many years ago, in an effective communication course the instructor said different employees are comfortable with different communication modes: some are comfortable with oral communication while others with written.

So if you insist all complaints be in writing, you will miss out on many who are more comfortable with oral communication.

Or if you like written complaints, would you put the complaint box so high that no one can reach it?

I know many of you think all this is trivial. But if we trivialize everything, we will not change and not become more helpful. We will become wilful or unwilful value starvers.

Some reasons why executives are not customer centric even though they are CX experts is their training and background:

1. Functional thinking:
    a. Being taught to be functional thinkers, in business schools and businesses
    b. Everyone has a job, and silo thinking is inculcated

2. No clear Customer Strategy. This leads to the following:
   a. The pursuit of profit, fueled by short-term results
   b. Not wearing their customer hat and wearing the company hat
   c. Thinking the company is not human, so the company does not need to appear human—It is an it
   d. Not geared toward problem solution

Functional thinking goes against the grain of Customer Value Creation. Why? Because, one is taught to do the defined job and not go outside the boundaries and create value. Very few people are able to create value in this circumstance as boundaries of their empowerment are defined and controlled. This is how silo thinking comes in.

Creating a customer strategy prevents all this. This assumes a proper customer strategy designed from the customer's viewpoint. That means thinking like the customer. Stop thinking like the company. Believe the company good and the customer good are similar and are not disassociated (or nonmiscible). Do not hide behind the fact that a company is supposed to be a nonhuman entity in law. Therefore, you believe you can hide behind the company's rules. Then you tell customers this is our rule, or did you not know our rules. Your biggest customers dictate their rules to you. You dictate your rules to whomever you can.

The Lowest Common Denominator

One would expect that foreign companies with highly touted service norms and quality would set a trend in India for better service and customer centricity.

Unfortunately, the bulk of the contribution is in terms of nicer looking offices, better salaries, but the service standards have slid to where their Indian competitors are. It seems as if companies are trying to get away with the bare minimum, so that, hopefully they are no worse than the Indian competitors. It is as if there is a quest to reach the lowest common denominator, and not achieve the highest service standards. Ray Kordupleski called the best of the people who reached the Lowest Common Denominator "the cream of the crap."

Gautam Mahajan

This is surely not right.

Lastly, problem solution outside the ones you have defined is not necessary. And so the customer gets starved of value.

Here are a few examples:

Citibank: I overpaid by a considerable amount on my Citibank Card. I wanted a refund for the overpayment. After 3 months of calling and writing to the grievance officer (who never deigned to reply), and likewise no response from the ombudsman, I got a call from someone in Chennai, wanting me to tell her my card number and my pin, which I refused to do. She said how I could expect a refund without giving her the information, which Citibank says is information we should never divulge. She then said I would have to tell her how I had paid the bill, by check or bank transfer, which bank, and so on.

I said call back for this information, and I never got a call. (Remember the system: The bank can call you but you cannot call them.)

> Most firms are great when things are going right, but try to get them to rectify a problem. That is an omigosh proposition for them.
>
> *Gautam Mahajan*

I gave up and quickly started to spend the money so that I would not need a refund (something Citi was hoping I would do in the first place, and drove me to it). Is this Value Starvation or Value Creation and for whom?

> Companies are set up to *sometimes* solve your problem, but they do not correct the systemic problem: It is the Not My Job syndrome, or worse, I don't care syndrome. Thus, the next customer has to face the same problem ...
>
> *Gautam Mahajan*

HP Ink: I bought the ink cartridge via HP home delivery. It did not work; so I called their service center to get a refund or replacement. They said I would have to bring the ink cartridge to their office because defective part requires us to bring it back personally to their office, negating a home delivery system. Next time I bought from Nehru Place in Delhi, and again the cartridge was defective...had to take it to the HP office, and they said exchange in 3 days. Four weeks went by before I got a replacement.

Note the Customer Value Starvation. I could not use my printer for 4 weeks. HP made me do more work for no fault of mine (except that I was unlucky to get a defective ink cartridge). Who cares?

Amazon: Amazon was to deliver an HP 934XL cartridge. Instead, I got three test cartridges (which are meant for initial installation of printer). They would not work on my machine because my machine was not in a start-up mode.

So I complained, explained the problem. Someone picked up the cartridge, and lo and behold I got a shipment of another three test cartridges! To cut a long story short, I finally asked for a refund, which I got in terms of a credit. In between I had talked to an Amazon executive, who did nothing.

Uber in India: The state of the taxis, (air conditioning not working, and premium taxis are the same as the non-premium ones) is sometimes not good. Uber Map does not work well. Safety is an issue. Some drivers use their cell phones while driving, and park away from the curb. And if you give bad comments you can get blacklisted by Uber.

A welcome change:

Nathu Sweets: I picked up chips from Nathu's store that turned out to be stale. I called 3 hours later and complained. No questions asked—we will replace the bag of chips within an hour with home delivery; we do not need to see the bill or collect the stale bag. This is Value Creation (some will call it delight) converted from Customer Value Starvation.

Lindt chocolates: Walter bought a box at Geneva airport. He brought it to Mumbai and opened it after 4 months. There seemed to be a white glaze on the chocolates, and he thought they had spoiled. He picked up the complaint card in the box and wrote to Lindt. In 2 weeks a replacement was sent. No questions asked. Walter has been a Lindt customer ever since.

Taj President: I was staying at the Taj President in Mumbai. On the way to the airport, I discovered I had left my laptop charger in my room. With great difficulty I got through to an executive. My question was have you found my charger, or at least, could you check. He asked if they found it, what would I want them to do with it. I said I wanted it sent to Delhi where I live. He said he would check how much a courier would charge and then I would have to pay by credit card before it was shipped. I was more interested in checking if they had found the charger.

But have you found the charger, I asked. No answer. He was more interested in how I would pay for shipping the charger if they found it. I hung up.

I then called the General Manager and explained the problem. He said let me find the charger and I will have it sent to the airport and put on the first plane going to Delhi. It will be delivered to your home. He called me a few minutes later and said they had found the charger and it is on its way to Mumbai airport!

The charger was delivered to my home in Delhi 4 hours later. A case of Value Starvation converted to Value Creation! And it created a loyal customer for Taj President.

In these examples, Customer Value Starvation is prevented by four *preventive measures*:

1. Proper, easy systems to deal with routine complaints, which may be minor
2. Training of staff, especially with customer contact, to be customer friendly
3. Frequent, random contact by top management with the ultimate consumer or user, so that there is direct feedback
4. Convenience and concern of the customer should always come before that of the company

Customer Value and Value Starvation

As we go past the Customer Value Starvation examples, we must understand in a better way Customer Value. This will help us make Customer Value a part and parcel of our offering to customers.

What Is Customer Value and How Can You Create It?

What Is and How to Use Customer Value?

Customer Value measures and tells us why a customer buys and why he rebuys or will buy more and from whom. It looks at the benefits a customer gets versus what it costs him for the product or service he buys from the possible competitors or sellers. If the customer perceives he gets more benefits than what he paid (total cost in price and non-price terms), value is created for him. And when he goes to buy, he compares the value created by competing products or services and buys from the company he perceives is creating the most value in this competitive world.

Companies are in business only because they have or can find customers who buy from them. Companies get and retain customers by creating value for them. The value we create depends on the customer's perception of the value.

Value has many different meanings. To some value means price (what is the value of this car?); to others it means benefit (the value I got from this car). It also means the worth of something. That is why you hear some people saying "value for money" (meaning they are price sensitive), and others who prefer "money for value" (meaning they are willing to pay for what they consider as benefits, as from a brand or a better product, or more convenience etc.) A definition is given here:

> Customer Value is the perception of what a product or service is worth to a Customer versus the possible alternatives. Worth means whether the Customer feels she got benefits and services over what she paid.

In a simplistic equation form, Customer Value is Benefits − Cost $(CV = B - C)$.

What the customer pays is not only price (cash, check, interest, payment during use, such as fuel and servicing for a car) but also non-price terms such as time, effort, energy, and convenience. Inconvenience could lead to Value Starvation and a loss of customer value.

The benefits include the advantages or quality of the product, service, image, and brand of the company or the brand of the product; the values the company and its people have; past experience; success one gets in using the product.

Values are different from Value (the plural of value as defined here is value). Values are what someone or a firm stands for: honesty, morals, ethics, sustainability, integrity, trust, and so on.

Consumers are distinct from Customers. Consumers use the product or the service, but may not buy the product/service. The value the consumer perceives influences the buying evaluation and perception of the decision maker or the customer. The customer is someone who buys or makes the decision to buy. A noncustomer is someone who could buy from us, but is buying from someone else.

How Is Value Created and What Does It Do?

Value is created just as much by a focus on processes and systems as much as it is by mindset and culture. Mindset and culture are much more difficult to change, and also difficult to emulate. It is easier to copy products and systems than to change mindsets and culture. Therefore, for long-term success, mindset and culture are important and lasting. These, along with systems, create great value and competitive advantage.

Value changes during the use of a product or during the Customer Journey. Value is perceived during the purchase intent, the shopping, the actual purchase or buying, the installation or start-up, the use, and even the resale. We sometimes call this the Waterfall of Needs (shown later). Needs change during the customer journey.

A good CX and satisfaction will create value for the customer. Creating Customer Value (better benefits versus price) increases efficiency, loyalty, market share, price and reduces errors. Greater market share and better efficiency leads to higher profits.

Customer Value Starvation is a cost to the customer and reduces the benefits. Thus, Customer Value Starvation reduces the value to the customer that companies are trying hard to increase.

How to Create Real Value

You first have to understand the Customer Value concept: what a customer perceives as value, how a customer's value needs change over time, and how to get customer feedback. You must realize that people buy a product or service that *creates the most value over competing options.*

To create real value, you must recognize what a customer perceives as value. You must comprehend how the customer views your competition's product. What is important to the customer in his buying decision? Is price more important or are benefits? Are you good at delivering what the customer believes is important? Are you able to deliver more than your competition on these factors?

I understand these are general terms, but they will help you to create value as you understand your customer's needs and perceptions. Let us look at some examples on how to create Customer Value:

1. Giving a price that makes the customer believe he is getting more than he pays for, in terms of the benefits, versus competitive offers
2. Reducing the price or keeping the same price and giving something extra over competition (this could be service, better attention, an add-on to the product)
3. Making it convenient for the customer to buy, and how he wants to buy and pay
4. Giving a proper price justification (or Value Proposition), not just a price
5. For dealers, the feeling the company will grow and offer new products for the dealers to sell; these are things that the dealer may not have an experience of, but they create value for the future
6. The image of the company, including the brand and the trust in the company, or when the customer appreciates the values of the company, including sustainability—these create value for the customer
7. Giving the customer a product that works as it is meant to (as perceived by the customer) and is easy for him to understand and use (so that no unnecessary time or energy has to be expended)
8. Making the customer feel valued; do not starve him of value

Making it easy for the customer to contact the company creates value, and an assurance that an answer will be given when and how promised

Waterfall of Needs

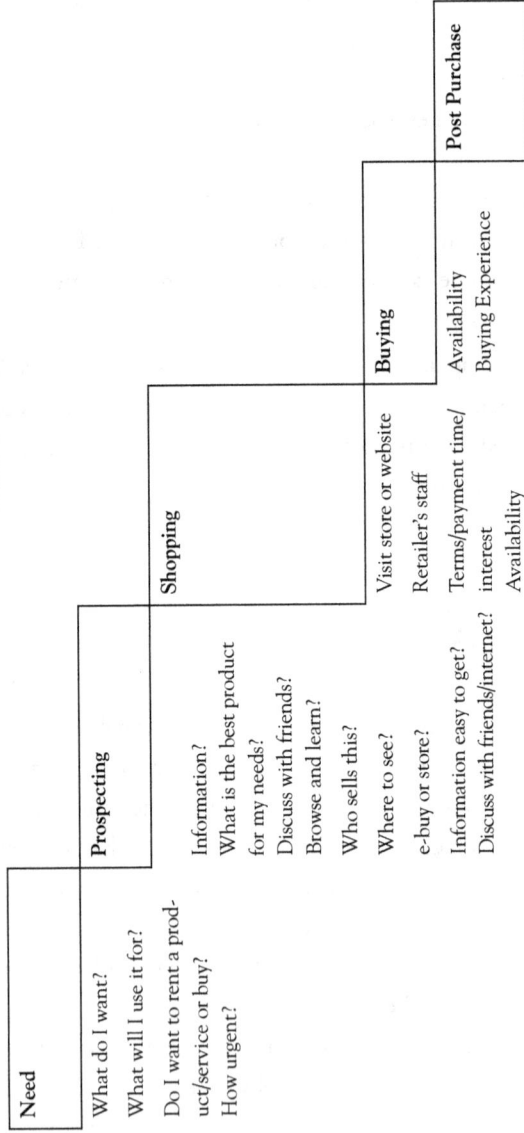

Need	Prospecting	Shopping	Buying	Post Purchase
What do I want?				
What will I use it for?				
Do I want to rent a product/service or buy?				
How urgent?				
	Information?			
	What is the best product for my needs?			
	Discuss with friends?			
	Browse and learn?			
	Who sells this?			
	Where to see?	Visit store or website		
	e-buy or store?	Retailer's staff		
	Information easy to get?	Terms/payment time/ interest	Availability	
	Discuss with friends/internet?	Availability	Buying Experience	

Non-price (do I need to assemble, pick up or free delivery, time of delivery, waiting time) Installation hassles is a non-price term

People I interact with
Information
Ease of getting credit
Availability and delivery time Billing
Speed
Retailer
E-tailer
Price
Non-price
Benefits versus cost or value

Delivery
Time taken to deliver
Availability/pick up
Service and service people

Use

Use experience | **After use**
Product | Repurchase
Service | intent
Cost | Loyalty/
Ongoing cost | Advocacy
Experience |

Waterfall of Needs: attributes we see

(how many times do you have to wait to talk to someone and how often does he promise to call back and how often do you get a call).

Not making you repeat questions or answers creates value and keep relating the problem

Receiving a call from a service person confirming his visit (the customer is not kept wondering whether the service visit will take place) creates value.

Not answering queries is a form of Value Starvation.

All readers have real-life examples of value creators and value starvers and can add many more examples. Do add yours. Answer the following:

> What could I do to create value for my customer?
> What can starve my customer of value? How do I avoid Customer Value Starvation?
> Does experience create value?
> List things that you do not experience that can create value for you.

Components of Customer Value

An easy way to understand Customer Value is to build an attribute tree to illustrate its components. Customer Value normally breaks up into Benefits (or utility) and the Cost. Usually, we build the waterfall of needs first, which is an outline of the customer journey.

Value breaks up into Benefits and Costs in the attribute tree given here:

Customer Value:	Benefits: X%	Product
		Service
		Image including Brand
		Emotional and Psychological Factors
		People
	Cost: Y%	Price
		Non-price

$X+Y=100\%$, X is the importance of Benefits and Y of Cost

Customer Value Starvation does not form part of and should not be a part of the attributes you want to give the customer.

Another method to understand the customer is to build a customer's waterfall of needs and derive the attributes from this. Note that Customer Value Starvation is not one of the customer's needs.

Measuring Value (Customer Value Added) and the Cost of Customer Value Starvation

Customer Value Added

Customer Value Added is our customer's perceived rating or score of the value we deliver divided by the perceived rating or score competition gets on the value they deliver to their customers. Where there is a transaction, we measure the memory of the experience and not the experience itself, (which is measured by using a satisfaction study with the user). So we measure value with the decision maker (not necessarily the user), and some time after the transaction.

To measure Relative Value Added, we need to do the following:

- Measure market perceptions of value our company adds
- Measure market perceptions of value added by competitors
- Define a relationship between the two

Customer Value Added

$$CVA = \frac{\text{Perceived worth of your offer}}{\text{Perceived worth of competitive offer}}$$

The Cost of Customer Value Starvation

Customer Value Starvation is an insidious loss to the company. The company does not even notice the loss.

It costs the company in many ways: It makes customers unhappy, causes customers to leave, and reduces loyalty.

The company has to work harder to correct problems caused by Customer Value Starvation and it is a cost to the company.

The employees are affected as they are often helpless in solving customer problems. There is a loss of efficiency and employee and customer happiness.

So, use the tools described in this book to find Customer Value Starvation and eliminate it. Make it a corporate objective and see how your business flourishes.

Value Deprivation

I have written about value destruction and how it can be turned into a value-creating opportunity. Value destruction assumes that value was or is available to you. Elsewhere, I have written about customer frustration when customers are value starved. But a more basic issue we as humans and marketers must look at is value deprivation.

What happens when value is not available to you because of circumstances or because you have no control?

Why is this important to companies and marketers? Very often, some people are deprived of common goods available to a higher economic class of consumers. Those who are being value deprived, use mud instead of soap; charcoal instead of toothpaste; have only one or no change of clothes instead of a wardrobe; have no recourse to quality or even minimum education; cannot get two square meals a day; have to work in someone's house and be deprived of an alternative future.

Many of these can be converted into opportunities, for example, through the sale of small bars of soap, shampoo and toothpaste sachets, or products with fewer features and a lower price point. I will leave the reader to think through these.

> Value deprivation occurs when you live in a village in India and have no opportunities. You reconcile yourself to this and do not want to do something or become someone. Then, we in big cities wonder why these people are that way and not ambitious.

Deprival value is based on the premise that the value of an asset is equivalent to the loss that the owner of the asset would sustain if *deprived* of that asset. So imagine the deprival value of a lost education or even poor education.

Much of this happens because people who can do something have closed their consciousness or trained it to ignore such things. Ayn Rand, in 1966, wrote in *The Voice of Reason: Essays in Objectivist Thought*:

> Men's consciousness is the least known and most abused vital organ...the loss of control of one's consciousness is the most terrifying of human experiences...and yet men abuse, starve and subvert their consciousness....She says this leads to the question, "Who is to blame? All those that are afraid to speak, or who know better and are willing to compromise, temporize and thus to sanction such happenings?"

Examples of Value Deprivation

Value deprivation occurs when you are clearly eligible to be selected for a national team, but because of vested interests or quotas you are not selected. Yet another example is a worthy candidate who cannot get admission to a good school because of reservations (his seat by merit goes to a poor person to provide the poor person with an opportunity). Or worse still, rich people who *bought* admissions for their kids to the detriment (deprivation) of deserving but less connected candidates.

An orphan, deprived of parental love is a case of value deprivation.

The case of workers being paid less than minimum wages in cash by greedy industrialists, who use their black money for this purpose and simultaneously deprive the workers of social benefits apart from paying lower wages, is also an example. During demonetization in India, these industrialists sacked the workers, depriving them of jobs, the economy of growth and then blamed their actions on the government. Had they been paying by check, this would probably not have happened.

A poor person who is unable to get recourse to justice or bureaucrats is value deprived. Do the clerks and the bureaucrats notice this?

A villager I met decided to send his son to Canada to prevent value deprivation in the village. They went to touts in a bigger city, who arranged admission in unknown colleges and with large payments. This is one consequence of value deprivation: making people do things out of desperation.

The worst example is the financial community, which in its greed has perpetuated great value deprivation in the guise of value creation. By making people who were marginal buy homes with cheap mortgages without worrying about the buyers' viability or the viability of the mortgages, they first deprived such people of long-term value and peace of mind, and finally, caused value destruction for them and society in a big way. (Value was destroyed for six million people who lost their homes and eight million people who lost their jobs as an aftermath of the 2008 financial crisis. No financial company officer had any value deprivation from this crisis or went to jail.)

Value deprivation is rampant in our legal systems, considering the long delays and the poor recourse to good lawyers, who are busy chasing high-paying crooks.

So What Can We Do?

The first and least is to become conscious and aware of value deprivation. Recognize it. Point this out in your circle of friends or your company.

Your innate ability may then suggest possible solutions for those you can impact or those your circle of friends and your company can.

A focus on value deprivation will increase value to people and society and improve the good and well-being of people all around.

Marketing people can look at their products that are deprived to people because of affordability, and they can come up with smaller sizes, lower feature products for such people and bring them into their fold.

This will all lead to reduction of value deprivation and increase value.

Look at Value Destruction as an Opportunity to Create More Value

Every act of creation is at first an act of destruction.

Pablo Picasso

Many companies analyze value destruction after the fact. Very few try to assess the value destruction potential of a new strategy, a new product, a new technology, or even a new hire, when they are looking at these. In the literature, the bulk of the papers are on analyzing value destruction after the fact.

Opposite thinking is a creative way to find an alternative solution to a problem.

This picture is taken with permission from Shep Hyken, "Opposite and Upside Down Thinking," https://hyken. com/customer-service-strategies/look-past-obvious-better-solution/attachment/opposite-and-upside-down-thinking/.

We suggest companies should discuss strategic risk to be studied up front. If organizations and the managers within them do so, they will be able to avoid or reduce the value destruction potential and in fact create much more value. Many companies learn their lessons or become smarter from analyzing value destruction that has already happened. This is the normal way companies have viewed value destruction.

Here, we are suggesting a hardly used technique: using, exploring, understanding, and evaluating value destruction possibilities to create more value. What we suggest is that during and after a strategy session or a review of a new project or a new product or service introduction, one should hold a session asking the following: In what way will this strategy, project, product, or service destroy value for me, my company, my customer, my employees, my partners, my society , or what is the potential for value destruction to occur, even if the destruction is a non-optimal solution.

The aim is to carry out an in-depth analysis of possible value destruction. Understanding the causes of value destruction or possible value destruction, one would then analyze how one could avoid such value destruction and actually create more value. Looking at solutions that are generally accepted and asking how they might destroy value can help us figure out better and more value-creating solutions. Many suggest that just reducing value destructing waste is not enough.

An Example: Strategy

Shareholder value destruction over 10 years showed that strategic risks were a major cause. This is because the strategic team does not look at risk and relegates this task to a risk evaluation team that did not have the *clout* to change thinking. We would like to expand this value destruction thinking to beyond risk and shareholder loss, but also to other potential problems. The example of smart lighting highlights this and is discussed later.

Along with pure strategic thinking, we also have to look at operational risk; compliance risk; political and regulatory risk. We are suggesting that this should not be done in a cursory fashion and just stating these risks have been looked at is not good enough, but to see what the company's leaders can do to mitigate these risks, reduce value destruction potential, and increase value creation potential. Chris Dann of Pricewaterhouse uses strategic risk to reduce strategic value destruction and create better value

The point is such value destruction should be foreseen and tackled in a serious manner.

One such thinking should be the impact of competitive disruptive moves. Companies should therefore embed value destruction and operational, regulatory, and political risk in their thinking. How could these happen? What can we do to prevent these from happening? In what way should our strategy change to reduce value destruction?

As an example, in earlier decades, we had business development people who were rewarded for bringing in new businesses. Many of them never worked on the new business they brought in, but were rewarded and moved on. I asked CEOs whether they rewarded business development executives for keeping them out of bad businesses. Most had not thought of this value destruction potential.

An Example: Smart Cities

1. Smart lighting: It is vastly understood and appreciated that smart lighting is the accepted approach for smart cities. While we agree, we also wish to examine what this means in terms of physical infrastructure.

   The typical way of using smart lighting is to put poles on roads and have lights that turn on when needed. This is all value creating. The following are potentially value destructing, however:

   a. Physical infrastructure: This is used less than 10 percent of the time. The cost of poles and the space required can be high. This is value destruction. So if we assume there is potential value destruction, what can we do? We could think of replacing pole-based lights by drones. Conceptually, 50 poles could be replaced by a smaller number of drones.

   The next thought is to look at using flying phones that can hover above the person walking, supplemented by fewer drones. Flying phones would belong to citizens and therefore be a smaller drain on the exchequer.

2. Physical transportation: Smart cities imply improvement of well-being of (or creating value for) citizens. Just giving sensor-based information is not enough. Value is destroyed because people have to live sometimes far from their place of work or schools or airports (and other transport hubs). One common example is moving from point A to point B in normal times and in times when tourists arrive in large numbers. The normal ride could be 20 minutes, but in the tourist season it could take as long as 2 hours. Perhaps a system of driverless cars and networked transportation or a ropeway is the added value over just better information. For example, the use of tubular transport as suggested by Elon Musk is important. An opposite thought is the concept of mass transportation be replaced by individual man–size transport systems.

3. People skilling: The next potential for value destruction in smart cities is that we do not have *smart* workers. Most current workers are untrained for this. This is a form of value destruction for the smart cities program and so these people should be skilled. For example, drone-handling skills, driverless car management skills are needed. Next, sensor-handling, sensor-troubleshooting skills may be needed. Therefore, skilling academies are required. Responsive urban governance should result in smarter value creation.

4. Self-healing and self-powering systems: Sensors and other devices can detect cracks or defects in concrete structures or in offices/homes. An analysis will reveal that intervention by humans is required to repair these defects. Perhaps, if we could use bio-concrete to self-heal cracks in concrete, we could create even more value. Lastly, biomaterials have a great future. These include self-healing polymer building materials, graphene, and the like and buildings that can change with temperature, or self-adjusting buildings.

Further analysis may show that energy loss or where energy is not easily available, that self-powering systems use could add more value and that reduce value destruction due to power loss. For example, solar power generation through solar layers on windows could add value.

There are other examples we can focus on:

Value destruction due to insolvency: The Indian Government brought in the Insolvency and Bankruptcy Code 2016 to make insolvency easier. An example of possible value destruction is given:

The potential for value destruction could occur if all the claimants were allowed to decide on the future of the company. Assured claimants would want their money fast and not worry about the value destruction to the company's net value. To avoid value destruction of this sort, strategically only those claimants who have a significant stake and risk in the well-being of the company should then be allowed to decide the fate of the company. Thus, people who design the law from a value creation (or least value destruction) point of view would have designed the law differently.

Value destruction due to short-term focus: It is well-known that short-term results and their reporting is a cause for value destruction in firms. A look at the value destruction potential would point out that companies must adopt a long-term view of their business, but the focus on stock prices and investor short-term gains obviates that. CFOs are encouraged to gain or manipulate numbers through accounting practices allowed under GAAP. Retail investors are more long-term investors and they are shortchanged by this thinking (value is destroyed for them). A proper study of value destruction would reveal that this practice has to be changed. An example is what Paul Polman of Unilever did: He told his shareholders he would only concentrate on long-term results and not short-term gains, and the result was spectacular for Unilever. Value is destroyed in yet another way by short termism: Lower returns mean lower investment, which hits the entire society.

Value creation and destruction of society from technology and artificial intelligence (AI): While this was the topic of a conference with the University of Kobe and the Japan Advanced Institute of Science and Technology in Kobe, Japan, October 14 to 16, 2019, it is germane to point out that technology development outpaces its absorption by society. Society is unable to adjust to technology quickly enough, causing short-term value destruction. In the long run, the danger of technology overtaking and controlling society is very real. Such value-destroying potential must be mitigated and reduced by strategic thinking by the owners and designers of technology, the designers of the recipient society, and all of us, in general.

Lastly, one value destruction potential of AI systems is when they do not respond to human commands. It might be possible to install a self-destruct system to circumvent such value destruction possibilities.

Value creation/destruction of plastic bottles: The Continental Group introduced the one piece plastic bottle as a source of large packaging (1 L, 2 L) for beverages. When they started work on the smaller sizes (half-litre or less), the can-making part of the business complained of value destruction for cans because plastics could possibly take over some of the market from cans.

Unfortunately, no one looked at the value destruction of the environment due to plastic waste. The risk analysis revealed that the risk would be minimal (meaning legislative and environmental) but ignored the problem of used bottles in the garbage stream. This is a classic case of value destruction.

The computer in the cockpit: The *Economist* and the *Times of India*, based on the Boeing crash in Ethiopia in March 2019, talked about aeroplanes flying in autopilot and with automated systems.

Humans struggle to cope when automation fails. What this means is that strategically and operationally we are working on automating transport systems and are training people in automation.

A study of this shows there is value destruction potential. This can be reduced by thinking through the following:

What do pilots do when automation fails or plays up?

How do we train on more manual controls in addition to the new training on computer control?

Today pilots spend more time learning automated systems and less time on hands-on flying. Newer pilots, who are more comfortable with automated systems, cannot handle manual systems as effectively as older pilots.

What is the optimum manual–automated control? Which one should override the other and when?

The perils of the human–machine interface can then be reduced. Note that perhaps a cost–benefit analysis showed the current system is acceptable. Studying the value destruction aspect would cause better training and operating techniques to emerge.

Adapted from Gautam Mahajan's article

Common Ways in Which Customer Value Starvation Is Created

The following two sections talk about ways companies commonly create Customer Value Starvation. By encouraging a Do Not Complain Culture, companies encourage Customer Value Starvation.

Don't Get on Our Wrong Side; and Do Not Complain

Digital Exile and Point of No Help

In this day of digital interaction, or interaction with low-ranking chat operators (call center operators for one) or chatbots, the customer has lost out and lost out big. Either things work for him, as they should, and he is satisfied or they do not. For big enough problems, he has little or no recourse to proper attention and quick interaction, because those who can solve problems are inaccessible to the customer, and he has to fend with chat operators or chatbots. The customer is put into Digital Exile, where he can only contact call centers or chatbots. You could call this Value Starvation.

Take the example of Jack Cunningham, who has gone into (in his own words) "Digital Exile: How I Got Banned for Life from AirBnB," https://medium.com/@jacksoncunningham/digital-exile-how-i-got-banned-for-life-from-airbnb-615434c6eeba. Read his remarkable experience. He objected to the owner walking in on them. (Has this happened to you? It happened to me in San Francisco, just after I came out of the shower; the owner had walked in. Luckily I had a towel tied around me. By the way I did not complain to AirBnB.) Jackson complained and gave the owner a low rating, and the owner came back by saying Jack was not AirBnB customer material.

What recourse does Jack have? Does anyone read what he says? Is all this condoned by people on the top who talk about giving a great experience?

Take Loic Ple: He wrote in the *Journal of Creating Value* about his experience with Amazon and being coerced by the Amazon partner to give a better rating before the Amazon partner would replace the part.

Loic gave a 1-star rating to a Chinese vendor for his malfunctioning earphones. In his words: She proposed to compensate for my poor experience by exchanging or refunding the earphones (without my sending back the defective ones, "so that I do not have to support any extra cost"). According to her e-mail, all I had to do was to reply if I agreed with this proposal—which I did, asking for another product to replace the previous one. The following day, I received another e-mail, which I was asked to forward to another mailbox with my order number, accompanied with the link towards the replacement product I could choose among a preselection made by the vendor. In the same e-mail, the vendor apologized several times once again, and ensured me that my case had been forwarded to the engineers so that the products are improved. I thus followed this procedure. The day after, I received a third e-mail that surprised me much more than the previous ones. This e-mail confirmed that I could place the order to receive a brand-new free product, but that first, I would have to either change or remove my 1-star comment on Amazon. Only after that would I receive the coupon for the free product (the exact sentence, translated from the French version of the message, was: "Would you be ready to help us by modifying your comment (to 4 or 5 stars) or to remove it given our after-sales service? We ask for your understanding and thank you for your kindness. All our customers can benefit from our after-sales service that would live up to their expectations. Once the comment is changed or removed, we will immediately send you a coupon"). After some hesitations, I eventually did that, and received my coupon to get my replacement product.

What do you do? Why can't the defective part be replaced? Whom do you go to for checking these pressure tactics?

Gautam had a similar problem with Amazon: They kept sending the wrong printer ink (happened three times on the same order), and that is when I canceled. No one cared I was getting the wrong ink. Who was high enough at Amazon to care, and how can I get to him? Never and impossible.

And my friend got a ride for his sister from Dwarka Colony to Delhi Cantonment Railway Station, some 16 km away. The taxi driver seemed to be going the wrong way, and when my friend's sister asked, the taxi driver said it was 200 km away and would not listen to her. In panic, she called her brother. The brother talked to the taxi driver and he refused to listen. He then tried to contact Uber (read my chapter on "The One Way Send: Receive Is Only for Payments"). Contacting Uber is impossible (I believe they now have a panic number to call). He finally called the police and then the taxi driver and told him of the police call. The taxi driver, turned around, dropped my friend's sister at Delhi Cantonment Station, and fled without any payment (in India, Uber accepts cash payments).

Take Bank of America. If you have a problem you can only call and if outside the country, it is an expensive proposition when the collect call number does not work, and you have to call by paying and being put on hold, and finally get incomplete information. When I called and disputed a debit, they gave me another 800 number to call. Welcome to the telephone loop!

All of you have examples. Where are the CX folks in the company preventing all this?

What can you and I do? Nothing, unless government legislates this. What about all the corporate people and consultants who talk and teach CX? Do they care? Or do they think the convenience of the company is more important than the convenience of the customer? Do they even teach this?

What can companies do? First, they need to examine if they truly want problems to be resolved. They must understand the problems customers are facing. They then can get to the problem resolution step. Companies have to prevent Value Starvation and find means to be responsive to customers.

Those of you in CX and at executive levels in companies should look within your companies and when you do, do help customers get in touch with you with no difficulty. Let customers reach you the way it is easy for them, and not how you dictate it. Respond to them fully. We all talk about doing the right things. This is your chance to differentiate your company. And as you start getting calls you will make an effort to solve such problems for everyone. When this happens, the number of calls will reduce as complaints will be less frequent.

Ask what customers value. They do not want to be anxious or worried about some aspect of dealing with you or their accounts. They want their grievances not only to be heard but be solved. The point is they want their problems to go away. As a company, you too want that. So start thinking about how problems can be solved, and thus go toward zero complaints.

Some countries have legislated ombudspersons to solve such problems. While a welcome move, these are cumbersome. Perhaps companies should have internal but independent ombudspersons, or better, grievance redressal systems.

Companies have to ask if they care, and if they do not, there is no solution.

Do add your examples and comments. Are you frightened by this? Has it happened to you? Will you be next?

Don't starve your customers of value.

One Way Send: Receive Is Only for Payments!

Have you noticed when dealing with companies, especially through the e-media, the company can get in touch with you? They contact you when they wish to (even when you don't want them to, with trivial questions like were you satisfied before the job was done!) But when you try to get in touch with them, you cannot, unless it is preordained by the company that you can contact them.

Typically, you can contact the company when you wish to buy or make a payment.

Then the company contacts you regarding the shipment. You can track the shipment. They send you a text message about delivery. We are delivering today. Heaven forbid, but you have a big meeting and won't be home, and neither is your neighbor…try contacting the company for the name of the delivery guy or his mobile number, or when precisely they will deliver…you cannot, or whether they can reschedule.

You then get a message—we were unable to deliver—and this goes on. Amazon once sent me a message my package was delivered, but it was never delivered, but how do I contact them? All they wanted was a satisfaction rating of the delivery.

Anytime you want to make contact beyond what the company will allow you, you cannot…you have only the rights we give you Mr./Ms. Customer. This is Customer Value Starvation.

Now this works great when there is no problem, and so companies have to hone the system to zero complaints and zero error. But zero contact is not to the customer's liking, especially when he wants to make contact.

For example, Amazon in India. The delivery guy came, but would not deliver because I was not present. He was told I would be back in 5 minutes. No, he cannot wait. When will he be back? Maybe tomorrow. There is no way to get any further information from the company but to play the waiting game.

I tried to get foreign exchange from Thomas Cook. You get on the Internet and ask for foreign exchange. Someone calls you, fixes a rate, and says he will call back…no call back, so you try calling the number the person had called from. No one picks up the phone. Then, out of the blue, I get a call. You will have to pay first. Thomas Cook will have to set up a payment portal. Can you pay right away? I say no, as I am driving. I am told he will call back in 30 minutes. No call and I cannot contact him. I get my forex elsewhere.

I just ordered Clorox on Amazon. It was to be delivered latest by April 4. Due to the Covid environment it was postponed to April 8. I then got around April 10 a request to rate the partner. But I had got no Clorox. So I looked at how to let Amazon know. They told me to contact the partner. They linked me, and they took all information but I could not send it to the partner (and of course, not to Amazon). That's the one-way connect syndrome creating Customer Value Starvation.

Why is the convenience of the customer not important? Why is creating Customer Value Starvation more important?

Learning Value from People on the Street

Walter says :

A one-man/woman business cannot afford to be just *takers*. They have to be primarily *givers*, who then benefit by taking.

Many of the lessons I have learned are from such businesses, where the CEO has not had the chance to distance himself from the customer.

The shoe shine boy, I have been using for perhaps 10 years, on Sir P.M. Road, Fort, Mumbai. When I stop for a shoe shine, he smiles. Asks me how I am. Not seen you for some time—he will add. Will give you a special polish today, with a new product, no extra charge. And he gets on with the job. He makes sure that my socks are not smeared with the polish. He will never complain about not having the right change. And when the job is done, there is a cheery goodbye—have a good day.

If my shoes are a new pair, he will compliment me. If he does not have the right shade of polish, he will rush to borrow it from a neighboring shoe shine person, and will do it fast. Anil is a *giver, not a taker*. A Value Creator.

The fruit vendor who comes with his cart every morning will phone my wife 15 minutes ahead, to take her order and then tell the prices and the total bill. By the time he comes to the house, he has the parcel ready and even the change, if necessary. Sometimes he will tell her, "I will get better bananas tomorrow," suggesting that she need not buy today. The weighing scale is accurate. There is no cheating.

No wonder we do not go shopping for fruits. Prem is a giver. Not a taker. He is a Value Creator who provides customer satisfaction.

I had informed three brokers about my office space in Panaji, Goa. I had wanted to sell it after 15 years to move to another space. It was at a prime location and in a prestigious building. One broker, Viegas, came back after 2 months with two good offers. They were in alignment with market rates. Then he asked whether his own company, which was growing, could buy this property for itself. There was a conflict of interest. But he liked it himself. And he would pay 5 percent more than the highest offer. I agreed. We shook hands. The next day I asked him to draw up the agreement so I could sign it before I left Goa. He did. And he informed me that he would not charge a broker's commission, since he was buying it himself. It would be a conflict of interest. I was impressed and also touched. I have had Viegas as my broker ever since. I trusted him. Viegas performed Value Creation.

A cab drove me from the hotel to Changi airport in Singapore. The fare was $23. I gave him $30. He returned $10. I said you have made a mistake— you gave me $3 more. He said he had brought me by a slightly longer route because part of the road to the airport was under repairs. Then keep that as a tip. No Sir, was the quick reply. We don't accept tips in Singapore. There was both apology and pride in his voice. It was Value Creation for Singapore public cabs.

On that same trip, after I had checked in for my flight, I felt the weight and rattle of the large hotel room key, which I had forgotten to return at the time of checking out. (They should have asked for it—but never mind.)

I now needed to post the key back to the hotel, before I left. When I went to the enquiry counter, the young lady told me that there is no post office at Changi terminal 2. But what is your problem? I explained to her. She gave me an envelope and told me to write the address, put the key in, and seal the envelope. Then put it in the post box near the Gucci shop down the corridor. What about the postage? Don't worry, she said. It will be delivered. A week later I got a thank you note from the hotel. The key was delivered. So much for Singapore postal services and customer satisfaction. In fact, it was Customer Delight!

Gautam adds, I had gone to Detroit for a meeting. The taxi dropped me from the airport to the hotel that night. The next morning, I noticed that my wallet was missing. I had no idea how to contact the cab or where I had dropped the wallet. My room was paid for so that was not a worry. Then I got a call from the taxi driver. That morning, while cleaning the cab, he had found my wallet in the crack at the back of the seat. He would pick me up, give me the wallet, and drop me to the appointment. He knew the hotel he had dropped me at, had called the hotel, and had found me. What great Customer Value!

How the Profit Motive Destroys Value

For years we have been discussing value destruction. A prime example of this is given in Francesca Mari's brilliant article on the cover of *New York Times Magazine* called "A $60 Billion Housing Grab by Wall Street." You can see it on:

https://www.nytimes.com/2020/03/04/magazine/wall-street-landlords.html

"Hundreds of thousands of single-family homes are now in the hands of giant companies—squeezing renters for revenue and putting the American dream even further out of reach," the article says.

Francesca describes a potential first-home buyer.

> When Ellingwood began speaking to lenders, he realized he could easily get a loan, even two; this was the height of the bubble, when mortgage brokers were keen to generate mortgages, even risky ones, because the debt was being bundled together, securitized, and spun into a dizzying array of bonds for a hefty profit. The house was $840,000. He put down $15,000 and sank the rest of his savings into a $250,000 bedroom addition and kitchen remodel, reasoning that this would increase the home's value.

For a variety of reasons including a divorce, he was unable to make payments on the mortgage and had to sell the house. The buyer turned out to be a finance company (almost like a private-equity company) who found this a lucrative market to invest in and squeeze higher profits from people who had meagre means.

Francesca writes,

> Before 2010, institutional landlords didn't exist in the single-family-rental market; now there are 25 to 30 of them, according to Amherst Capital, a real estate investment firm. From 2007 to 2011, 4.7 million households lost homes to foreclosure, and a million more to short sale. Private-equity firms developed new ways to secure credit, enabling them to leverage their equity and acquire an astonishing number of homes.

You have to read the article to see the disregard for the customer in preference to make more money. The convenience of the company comes before the convenience of the customer. And sadly, this happens to a bunch of customers who mostly can barely afford to pay the mortgage and are not able to do any major (and often minor) repairs. The story is one of greed and making the purpose of a company to generate more money, and not worry about creating value for the stakeholder (the customer, the employees, partners, and society).

Thus, a society meant to be one where people can get affordable housing could not exist for all because of such greed.

The private-equity model that Francesca talks about, in general, prioritizes short-term earnings and harvesting as much money as possible even if it means destroying value rather than building a solid company that creates values and results in long-term earnings.

All this could be a repeat of the 2008 financial crisis, which damaged the economy and those who were marginal home owners. Her article is a wake-up call for companies and governments to create value for people in the marginal category who have no choice but to rent.

This greed is how the economy collapsed in 2008. And this is being repeated. The problem emanates from a business strategy that tells the companies they can make more money by playing out the strategy. There is no customer strategy to ensure the customer is focused on and his well-being is important.

One solution is developing and following a Customer Strategy.

For a long time, I have been advocating to CEOs that the starting point of a good business strategy is a customer strategy. The customer strategy and the shareholder strategy should then be used to build a business strategy/business tactics. And in today's age both the business and the customer strategy should be adaptive to the changing future.

To many, customer strategy can appear to be redundant. But it isn't. It is crucial if organizations want to change and become truly customer centric. A survey of 400 CEOs showed that 33 percent felt that the number one issue in preventing customer centricity was a lack of a clear customer strategy. Twenty-eight percent felt it was internal silos. Customer strategy helps break silos and creates teamwork. This happens because CXOs are part of creating the strategy. They therefore are part of the customer strategy. They assign customer roles for themselves and their departments.

They agree to lead certain customer-related strategies. They become part of the customer-focused team. And as key performance indicators (KPIs) include customer parameters, the customer strategy becomes a practical road map to build customer value and create value for the customer.

Strategy must build competitive advantage for the firm by creating compelling value for customers. Articulating why customers will buy requires managers to examine strategy from the customer's point of view. It encourages them to ask how the firm's activities deliver superior value to chosen customers. The firm must choose the set of activities that serve target customers better than competitors, and shun other segments that demand incompatible activities. This is what a customer strategy will do for a company.

Many people ask me the difference between a customer strategy and a business strategy. They cannot see the difference since the business strategy is based on the marketplace. The customer strategy looks at the customer, his needs, and the customer opportunity. The difference can be seen from what happened in the recent meltdown of the financial markets, starting with the mortgage market crash.

The typical mortgage customer was looking for a product that would keep him safe if the prices of homes went down or interest rates went up. The mortgage company should pay attention to the customer's liquidity and ability to pay. A customer strategy would have revealed the customer's needs and also suggested what products needed to be created to make the mortgagee safer if prices of homes went down or interest rates went up.

The market opportunity that arose was to bundle mortgages and sell them to a bigger financial institution, thereby getting money back to give out more mortgages. These new mortgages were then bundled and resold from a bigger financial institution to an even larger one. The buyer of these bundled mortgages bundled more of them and sold them on to the next larger financial company. The mortgagee was no longer the real concern of the original mortgager. The paper was held somewhere else.

As you can see, the business strategy of bundling mortgages was a great idea to make money.

No one was concerned about the quality of the mortgagee and the loan. They were too busy fulfilling their business strategy of bundling mortgages and offloading them to the next person.

And what was the result? The mortgage market collapsed, because everyone took their eyes off the customer and did not have a clear-cut customer strategy, though they had a business (market-based) strategy. Often the customer was not worthy of a mortgage.

Customer strategy, specifically data intelligence, is at the forefront of one bank's effort to be customer centric:

- How can I stand out from competitors in a crowded and volatile industry?
- Who are customers? Who are my target customers?
- What do my customers value so I can provide them the value they seek?
- Are we creating more value than competition? If yes, then where and how? How do we improve?
- Should I concentrate on customer acquisition or focus on share of wallet?
- What can I promise customers and how do I keep promises?
- What additional value can I create for customers, and those that serve them?
- How do I find actionable insights from internal and external data?
- How do I organize to focus on customers?
- How do I implement customer programs?
- Who leads specific programs?
- What will the future be? How will our customers change, and how should we?

Customer strategy also allocates customer tasks to various departments, breaking silos and making all departments have a responsibility for the customer. This builds teamwork, builds the customer priority and focus in all departments. Key performance areas can then be customer based and incentivized. This is an extremely important reason for the customer strategy being built.

The customer strategy can then be a precursor to the business strategy.

You can see none of this was part of the corporate thinking in Francesca's article. And the state that was to monitor the well-being of the citizens abrogated their responsibility to greedy landlord companies.

Companies and governments must have a customer strategy to take care of their constituents. All this might sound like wishful thinking by companies, but customers are in their long-term interest and they should avoid short-term money-making schemes.

SECTION 2

Customer Value Thinking

The Revised Purpose of a Company Is to Create Value for All Stakeholders

Value Starvation has become important especially after the Business Roundtable announcement in August 2019, where CEOs of the top 300 companies in the United States signed off on the new Purpose of a Company.

Statement on the Purpose of a Corporation as Stated by the 300 Corporate Leaders in the Business Roundtable, August 2019

Americans deserve an economy that allows each person to succeed through hard work and creativity and to lead a life of meaning and dignity. We believe the free-market system is the best means of generating good jobs, a strong and sustainable economy, innovation, a healthy environment, and economic opportunity for all.

Businesses play a vital role in the economy by creating jobs, fostering innovation, and providing essential goods and services. Businesses make and sell consumer products; manufacture equipment and vehicles; support the national defense; grow and produce food; provide health care; generate and deliver energy; and offer financial, communications and other services that underpin economic growth.

While each of our individual companies serves its own corporate purpose, we share a fundamental commitment to all of our stakeholders. We commit to:

> **Delivering value to our customers:** We will further the tradition of American companies leading the way in meeting or exceeding customer expectations.

Investing in our employees: This starts with compensating them fairly and providing important benefits. It also includes supporting them through training and education that help develop new skills for a rapidly changing world. We foster diversity and inclusion, dignity and respect.

Dealing fairly and ethically with our suppliers: We are dedicated to serving as good partners to the other companies, large and small, that help us meet our missions.

Supporting the communities in which we work: We respect the people in our communities and protect the environment by embracing sustainable practices across our businesses.

Generating long-term value for shareholders, who provide the capital that allows companies to invest, grow, and innovate. We are committed to transparency and effective engagement with shareholders.

> A young American coming out of Satyajit Ray's movie *Distant Thunder*, about the famine in Bengal in 1943, says to his companion: "I did not know that people can die of starvation."
> A case of becoming aware.
> *Your customers too can die of Value Starvation.*

Each of our stakeholders is essential. We commit to deliver value to all of them, for the future success of our companies, our communities, and our country.

Thus, the statement adopted in New York in 2019 goes beyond Peter Drucker's oft-repeated dictum—"The only purpose of a company is to create and keep customers"—although this dictum still remains the foundation for all our businesses.

When Will We Ever Learn: Why the Revolution in Corporate Complaint Handling Has Failed So Far

by Marc Grainer, Scott M. Broetzmann, and David Beinhacker

Marc Grainer is Chair, Scott M. Broetzmann is President & CEO, and David Beinhacker is Chief Research Officer, Customer Care Measurement & Consulting

Background

Before the 1980s, most American companies viewed such customer care initiatives as responding to complaints as a necessary evil, at best, and as a significant administrative cost, at worst. Companies all too often approached complaint handling as an adversarial process where they were pitted against *unreasonable* customers and *anti-business* regulatory agencies.

The focus was generally on narrow legal issues. Most efforts were directed toward rebutting individual customer claims and heading off additional consumer protection regulation. Many companies viewed complainants as trying to take unfair advantage of business, rather than as customers whose continued brand loyalty and positive word of mouth could be a valuable marketing asset.

During this same time frame, consumer advocacy groups likewise followed a legalistic strategy. They concentrated their efforts on the adjudication of individual customer claims and on strengthening the consumer protection regulatory framework (e.g., during the mid-1970s, consumer groups supported the establishment of a consumer protection agency at the federal level). They viewed business with suspicion and, as a general rule, felt that the legal system, not the marketplace, was the best forum for resolving customer problems.

With the advent of the *Reagan revolution* in the 1980s, however, there was a major reassessment by business of its approach to handling customer complaints. During the past 30-plus years, the adversarial/regulatory point of view has largely been replaced by marketplace/profit center considerations. Instead of litigating *who's right and who's wrong,* companies now tend to concentrate on *being number one in customer satisfaction.* Instead of hiding from complaints, many businesses now actually solicit them. What was once viewed as a nuisance/cost center is now typically thought of as a powerful retention marketing strategy. This increased priority given to corporate complaint-handling practices constituted a major element of the customer care revolution that emerged in the United States during the last quarter of the twentieth century.

The White House Study

Research initiated by the Nixon administration made a significant contribution to this change in business practice. During 1974, Special Advisor to the President and Director of the U.S. Office of Consumer Affairs, Virginia Knauer, commissioned a study that investigated how companies handled customer complaints. The main focus of this research (the White House Study) was a national probability survey of 2,513 households conducted in 1976.[i] These interviews were administered in the respondents' homes. This survey profiled the problems American households experienced with products/services and examined customer complaining behavior.

The finding from the White House Study that initially caught business's attention was the existence of a positive relationship between complaining and continued brand loyalty. As Table 1 illustrates, this relationship applied even when complaints were not satisfactorily resolved. Evidence of this was the fact that dissatisfied complainants with both serious (more than $100 financial loss) and relatively minor ($1 to $5

---

[i]For a detailed description of the findings from this survey, see A National Survey of Complaint- Handling Practices Used by Consumers, NTIS PB-263-82 (Washington, D.C.: U.S. Office of Consumer Affairs, 1976)

Table 1 Brand loyalty uplift: White House Study

Uplift in brand loyalty from non-complainants to...	Minor problems	Serious problems
Satisfied complainants	+33%	+44%
Dissatisfied complainants	+9%	+9%

Note: In the White House Study, satisfaction with the action taken to resolve complaints was measured using a five-item, ordinal word scale. Satisfaction was defined by the top three boxes ("received more than I asked for," "completely satisfied," and "not completely satisfied but the solution was acceptable"). Dissatisfaction was defined by the bottom two boxes ("not completely satisfied but I did get something" and "not at all satisfied").

financial loss) problems reported brand loyalty uplifts in the range of nine percentage points when compared with the loyalty of customers who didn't complain about their problems.

The fact that the White House Study found most complaints were not satisfactorily resolved (only 44 percent of complainants felt that their expectations were exceeded, were completely satisfied, or that the resolution was acceptable) didn't dampen business's newfound enthusiasm for complaint handling. On the contrary, the "Hawthorne-like" effect, identified by this study, where incremental brand loyalty was gained even when complaints were handled ineffectively, provided business with a kind of marketing "free lunch" that applied to 56 percent of all complainants.

The greatest marketing payoff, though, was the uplift in brand loyalty between non-complainants and those who were satisfied. Here satisfied complainants with serious problems reported an uplift of 44 percentage points while there was a 33 percentage point uplift for those experiencing minor problems.

Product/service problems have always been a major contributor to customer churn. These data from the White House Study suggested that complaint handling could be an effective strategy for keeping customers who otherwise would have been lost. Few marketing campaigns can claim credit for the magnitude of the incremental increase in brand loyalty resulting from satisfying complainants.

The White House Study further found that satisfying complainants could result in quite desirable return on investments (ROIs). The study also concluded that, whether in growth or mature industries, the cost of keeping existing customers was less than finding new ones. These findings, plus the incremental brand loyalty uplift data, became major justifications for business's newly found interest in proactively soliciting complaints.

As the *Washington Post* reported in her October 30, 2011 obituary:

> ...Mrs. Knauer showed that it was good business to cater to consumers. She commissioned a study...demonstrating that companies could prosper more through good customer relations than by attracting new customers through advertising.

The U.S. Office of Consumer Affairs made promotion of this finding the centerpiece of its agency mission from the Ford through the Reagan administrations.

This reevaluation of the worth of complaint-handling practices led corporate America to invest billions of additional dollars in this area. Inbound customer care call centers, policy adjustments beyond warranty limits, satisfaction surveys, upgraded customer-facing employee training programs, and the assignment of customer relations managers to retail outlets are examples of the expanded customer friendly initiatives adopted by business. The assumption of business was that this investment would improve corporate complaint-handling practices and thereby increase the percentage of satisfied complainants.

The question is did business reap the rich marketing benefits promised by the White House Study as a result of the increased priority given to corporate complaint-handling practices?

The Customer Rage Studies

Introduction

Customer Care Measurement and Consulting, LLC (CCMC), in conjunction with the W.P. Carey School of Business, Arizona State University (ASU), has conducted a series of six follow-up studies (interviewing a total of 6,114 U.S. households) to determine if the promise of upgraded corporate complaint-handling practices suggested by the original White House Study has actually been fulfilled. These telephone surveys (Customer Rage Studies), fielded from 2003 to 2013, replicated the core questions from the original 1976 study and explored such additional issues as

Table 2 Brand loyalty increase/decrease: Customer Rage Studies

Increase/decrease in brand loyalty from non-complainants to…	Minor problems	Serious problems
Satisfied complainants	+21%	+20%
Dissatisfied complainants	-12%	-12%

Note: The dissatisfied response categories to the satisfaction with the action taken to resolve complaints question used by the Customer Rage Studies differed from those used by the White House Study in two aspects. First, the fourth box response category used the terminology "but some action was taken" instead of "but I did get something." Second, a sixth response category was added: "I was not at all satisfied because no action was taken." Those responding to this bottom item were coded as dissatisfied complainants.

customer rage and the fulfilment of remedy-related expectations.[ii] (Both the White House and Customer Rage Studies focused on the most serious product/service problems experienced by the households during the year preceding these surveys.)

The follow-up Customer Rage Studies have produced a little *good news* and a whole lot of *bad news*.

Does the Relationship between Complaining and Brand Loyalty Reported by the White House Study Still Hold True Today?

Over the past 30-plus years the positive relationship between complaining and increased brand loyalty has become *conventional wisdom* in the customer care field. The more recent Customer Rage Studies, however, report that only half the original brand loyalty uplift paradigm still applies.

As Table 2 indicates, the brand loyalty uplift between non-complainants and dissatisfied complainants no longer exists. On the contrary, for both

---

[ii]The results of the first Customer Rage Study were released in 2003 in the Customer Care Alliance working paper, Grainer, Marc, Broetzmann, Scott, and Cormier, Cynthia; "Customer Complaint Handling – The Multibillion Dollar Sinkhole" and in Grainer, Marc, Broetzmann, Scott, and Cormier, Cynthia, "Checkmate: Complaint Handling at an Impasse with Rage," Customer Relationship Management, pp. 12 – 16, October, 2003, Volume VIII, Number 5. In recent years, CCMC has released the results of the Customer Rage Studies at ASU's Compete Through Service Symposiums (e.g., In 2013, "Will We Ever Learn?: The Sad State of Customer Care in America"). A detailed presentation comparing findings from 2015with those from the previous six waves of the Customer Rage Studies can be found at www.customercaremc.com. The eighth wave of the Customer Rage Studies is being fielded during the summer of 2017.

serious[iii] and minor[iv] problems, the Customer Rage Studies report that dissatisfied complainants are now 12 percentage points less brand loyal than non-complainants.

The bad news, then, is that the marketing "free lunch" identified by the White House Study is over. It now no longer pays, in added loyalty, for business to handle complaints ineffectively.

While the second half of the incremental brand loyalty uplift paradigm (the benefits resulting from satisfying complainants) still applies, the magnitude of this marketing advantage is substantially diminished. Now the marketing uplift for satisfied complainants is only 21 and 20 percentage points for minor and serious problems, respectively.

Therefore, the good news is that business can still gain a marketing advantage by satisfying complainants. The bad news is that simply soliciting complaints, without satisfying the complainers, no longer makes economic sense. Today, then, it is necessary for business to maximize the percentage of satisfied complainers for corporate complaint-handling practices to earn a meaningful ROI.

Has Business's Added Investment in Corporate Complaint Handling Led to Increased Complainant Satisfaction?

In order to most effectively exploit the true promise of the White House Study, complainant satisfaction needs to be significantly higher than the level reported in the mid-1970s, when less than half of complainers were satisfied with business's efforts to resolve their product/service problems. The most disappointing finding and biggest surprise from the Customer Rage Studies is that complainant satisfaction has actually decreased. After spending literally billions of dollars to improve corporate complaint-handling programs over the past 30-plus years, satisfaction has dropped to 41 percent compared with 44 percent in 1976. This means that the early promise of upgraded corporate complaint-handling practices remains largely unfulfilled.

[iii]The 1976 "more than $100" financial loss figure corrected for inflation is more than $400 today.

[iv]The 1976 $1 to $5" financial loss figure corrected for inflation is $1 - $20 today.

Table 3 What complainants wanted versus what they got in 2013:
Double Bupkis

Remedy	% Wanted	% Got
To be treated with dignity	94%	35%
An assurance that my problem would not be repeated	84%	21%
Offending company put itself in my shoes	83%	23%
My product repaired/service fixed	81%	31%
An explanation of why the problem occurred	81%	23%
A thank you for my business	80%	33%
An apology	76%	32%
To be talked to in everyday language; not scripted response	76%	32%
Just to express my anger/tell my side of the story	68%	37%
My money back	52%	21%
A free product or service in the future	41%	14%
Financial compensation for my lost time, inconvenience, or injury	40%	10%
Revenge	20%	3%
Other	12%	3%

Note: Shading indicates nonmonetary remedy.

With this in mind, the next question to be addressed is, why haven't business's efforts over the last 30 years led to increased complainant satisfaction?

Possible Explanations Why Complainant Satisfaction Hasn't Increased

Bupkis and Double Bupkis

Three sets of factors influence the level of complainant satisfaction: process (first contact resolution, timeliness of response, customer care agent performance, etc.), external factors (severity of customer problem, state of the economy, cost of the offending product/service, damages caused by customer problems, etc.), and remedy. While process and external factors certainly have an impact on satisfaction, CCMC's research suggests that remedy is by far the most important determinant of complainant satisfaction.[v]

---

[v] See CCMC's 2011 working paper, Broetzmann, Scott, Grainer, Marc, and Beinhacker, David, "Why the Customer Care Revolution has Failed: The Fallacy of Conventional Wisdom."

The best way to describe the remedies received by complainants from the Customer Rage Studies is to use the Yiddish expression *bupkis*.[vi]

Complainants were asked whether they had got any relief as a result of contacting the offending business. In 2013, 56 percent responded that they "got nothing" as a result of complaining. In other words, they got *bupkis*.

The remaining 44 percent of complainants were read an exhaustive list of both monetary and nonmonetary remedies and asked if they had wanted, and if so, whether they had got any such relief. As Table 3 illustrates, these complainants felt that business had given them relatively little for their efforts.

There was minimal monetary relief, such as a refund, reported or getting the offending product repaired/service fixed. Further, and most surprising, such nonmonetary remedies as apologies or explanations as to why the problem had occurred were likewise in short supply.

Therefore, it's likely many of those complainers responding that they had got something may have felt they ended up with *double bupkis*—a lot of effort for very little return. It is difficult to imagine how complainant satisfaction would increase given the *bupkis*-like remedies being offered by business.

[vi]The literal translation of "bupkis" means nothing.

Customer Value Starvation and Business Thinking

by Paul Selby

Raising the customer experience bar by mapping unexpected journeys
Paul Selby is Product Marketing Director for ServiceNow

The opportunities for companies to provide amazing customer experiences are plentiful; the unfortunate fact is they are often overlooked. In this story, that's not the case.

I faced a dilemma recently. I had ordered something that would be delivered while I was out of town. Normally this wouldn't be an issue: Someone would eventually be home to retrieve the package from the porch. The problem was this was a valuable item and the package might sit for hours. With the holidays approaching making porch pirates a larger threat, I thought I'd see if any options might exist to address my concerns.

Like most customers, I started my quest online to see if I could find a solution to my problem. I tried the vendor first, but they didn't offer any options once the item had left the warehouse. Then I tried the shipper.

This particular shipper is one of the *big two* in the United States, UPS. While I have used them to ship the occasional package, I was not familiar with all the services they offered. I was pleasantly surprised to discover I had a few options for my situation: delay delivery to another day of my choice for a nominal fee, hold at one of their local facilities for pickup, or have it delivered to a lockbox I could access 24 hours a day. I opted for the third option, figuring I could pick it up on my way home from the airport.

This ended up being a very effortless process. I arrived home from the trip package in hand and a very satisfied customer—a happy ending! This would not have been the result had the shipper not done four things.

Identify Exceptions

A delivery company's primary job—their contribution to the customer journey—is to get packages from point A to B. Granted, this is by no means an easy task when all the nuances of moving boxes around the world are considered. Still, it's just one part of the purchase process for the buyer in the overall journey they are on.

At some point, this shipping company had recognized their role wasn't always a straight line. Events occur in people's lives that can disrupt this process. A real concern is the security of a package when someone won't be available to receive it. They had identified this and determined they could address it.

Give Options

Realizing that the customer journey isn't always direct and simple is a positive first step. From there, they could have chosen to offer one alternative to address the situation, effectively force fitting an option that might not work for every customer. Even if slightly inconvenient, that one option would be preferable to a lost package, after all.

The shipping company instead offered three alternatives. Perhaps the customer wasn't sure when they would be home for a delivery. Perhaps they didn't want to incur additional charges. All possible concerns that might arise for a customer in this situation were addressed.

Automate and Inform

My first inclination was to go online for a solution. Not only did I find the answer I was looking for, but each of the options could be initiated directly from the website—no need to call, e-mail, or chat with customer service. In addition to redirecting the package, I was able to not only subscribe to regular text message updates as to the success or failure of the redirect but also a confirmation message once the package was available for pickup in the lockbox.

Customers go online for customer service because it's available any-time and anywhere and they can address problems at a time convenient to them. It's no wonder why customers prefer self-service. If a customer needs to make changes to an order or a delivery due to unexpected cir-cumstances, this shipper was keeping their experience positive by making actions as simple as a few clicks or taps and providing them with proactive updates to ensure they stay informed.

Trustworthy

I had never tried using an option to delay and redirect a package delivery. Though we live in the twenty-first century, one part of me thought it was somewhat risky to attempt to redirect a package already en route. While the package had a tracking number and was insured, still if it were lost in transit that would be just as inconvenient as it being stolen.

What overcame these concerns was the shipper's excellent reputation. They are a brand respected worldwide for their package delivery and lo-gistics solutions. More than half of the items I order online are delivered by them and over many years they have earned my respect and trust. Despite my concerns, their reputation took away the reluctance I had in taking this alternate path. I would probably have tried to arrange for someone to be at my house the originally planned day of delivery if this were not the case.

Going beyond What's Expected

In e-commerce transactions, the shipper is really just a middleman, one of the steps in the overall customer journey. For this particular shipping company, what makes its contribution unique are the steps it took to en-sure customer delight and a favorable outcome despite disruptions to the standard delivery process.

I had already had many prior positive experiences with this shipper. This event further cemented them in my mind as the first choice when either having a package shipped to me or shipping something myself.

Companies like this that consider the exceptions that occur in their customers' journey and have easily accessible remedies available are the companies customers will appreciate and reward with loyalty and positive referrals.

Walter's comments: These companies care for their customers, and do not ignore the oddball. Create Customer Value not Starvation.

Who the Hell Is the Customer?

Twenty-three years ago Walter wrote a landmark article, "Who the Hell Is the Customer?" This is reproduced here. It seems that not much has changed in 23 years. Unfortunately, because we need to change.

Sometime ago there was one day strike by all employees of the General Insurance Corporation. What did they want? Higher wages? Better working condition? Better training? Greater opportunities to contribute? None. They were protesting against the government's intention to open up the insurance sector to private and international companies. They probably feared that these new companies will charge lower premia, settle claims promptly, and pay higher compensations. All this is good for the consumer who now sometimes has to wait a long time for his claims to be settled or has to go from pillar to post and through endless correspondence and meetings at higher and higher levels to get what is his due in the first place!

The proposed Tata SIA Airlines is in trouble. It seems a good project. Most airline travelers are happy that such a project has been conceived and proposed. Airline projects have to be of a certain size in order to be viable as recent experience has shown. Consumers have seen the performance record of SIA on the international routes. Some among them remember the days when Tatas ran the airlines themselves and their customer-oriented approach. They have heard about how JRD travelled on Air India in an emergency and took whatever seat was available. And how he insisted on everyone else being served and took umbrage at any special consideration being shown to him.

Consumers have also seen how Air India, in spite of running up large losses, has still approved of free tickets for present, past and future directors of the airline, and first class seats too!

The arguments used by the government is that Tata SIA will further adversely affect the working of Indian Airlines and will affect the jobs of the disproportionately large number of employees who have found shelter under the large umbrella of a less than efficient "public sector" enterprise.

On a visit to the US, I could change my flight schedule on Delta and reconfirm this on the telephone. They made it so convenient and easy.

But on another visit to Rome, when I phoned the Air India office to reconfirm my flight back to Mumbai, they said the flight had been cancelled. The plane was allotted to the prime minister for his visit to China. I could be accommodated in another flight leaving Rome 2 hours later on the same day that would stop en route at Paris and arrive in Mumbai 5 hours later than scheduled. I had no choice. Could they please confirm my seat on this flight?

No way. Not on the telephone. I would have to come to the Air India office with the ticket and have the seat confirmed. I spent half a day doing this—and missing out on half a day of attendance at a World Conference which I had gone to attend, spending a considerable amount of time and money.

The airline had to look after the needs of the prime minister. It had to look after the convenience of the Air India office staff.

A nationalized bank started a branch at Chembur 25 years ago with much fanfare. The branch manager personally went from house to house of prospects, requesting them to open an account at this new branch. He said they will do their best to orient their services to customers. And they did. The staff was courteous.

Action was taken fast. The timings were designed to suit suburbanites in Mumbai who generally leave the house at 8 a.m. and return at 7 p.m. So the bank opened at 7.30 a.m. and closed at 8 p.m. with a long lunch break in between. The branch did well and then the staff forgot the very lessons that made the branch successful. The female staff complained that it was no longer safe to go home after 8 p.m. That the 7.30 a.m. opening time was too early. And they shifted to the standard bank timings. The bank manager and his successors succumbed to pressure from employees, rather than doing what was best for the customer.

(Now the newer banks do. Times Bank started a branch in Chembur and keeps it open on Sundays!)

There was a crowd jostling and shouting at the Chembur railway station a few weeks ago. The ticket counter was closed beyond the time specified for lunch. The staff member was there—but he was chatting with colleagues and having a cup of tea. The more restive the crowd became, the more he tested their patience. Finally, he began issuing tickets 10 minutes after the appointed time. Commuters In the queue missed four trains during that period. But the ticket staff had demonstrated their power. "If you want a ticket, you will have to wait. We should not appear subservient to the commuter. We work for the government—not for the consumer."

We get a telephone bill for 10 times our monthly average. We know there has been an error especially since we have been out of town for one and a half of the 2 months for which we have been billed.

I go to the MTNL office to complain. "Yes, we will look into it," they say, "but first you must pay the bill. You can claim a refund later, if this is found justified." MTNL is a monopoly. A government monopoly at that. Its primary objective is to enlarge itself into a monolith and provide employment. The customer is incidental.

The consortium of taxi drivers at Goa Airport have got used to charging unduly high fares for the ride from the airport to wherever you want to go. The minimum acceptable is Rs. 300. Damania Airways (late lamented) understood the problem of consumers and introduced a bus service from the airport to Panjim city. A fair charge was made. It was a boon to passengers who travelled by Damania. But the good days did not last long. The taxi drivers stoned the bus. They made it difficult to operate the service. Neither the government nor the airport authorities nor the airport police intervened. The taxi drivers continue to take passengers "for a ride."

Peter Drucker, the high priest of management, keeps repeating that "the purpose of the existence of a company is to create and keep a customer." Poor man. We are proving him wrong!

Value Destruction and Zero Complaints

Sometimes, companies have (like women's hair color) many alternatives.

A store or a company may not be able to predict all the colors needed, and sometimes may have too many of one colour and none of a slow-moving colour....This is a form of Starvation.

A person at a desk servicing customers may have three states:

1. No customer in line, and the company loses money
2. Just the right number so the wait time is optimum
3. Too many customers, with an inordinate wait time...the latter starves customer of their time

The first one is bad for the company.

What should companies do?

1. Withdraw slow-moving colors?
2. Not man the desk when few customers are anticipated?
3. How to manage all this so that the customer sees no Starvation?

Contrast with wilful starvation:

Come back tomorrow—or worse—

not providing telephone numbers or e-mail addresses, and no procedures in place to solve customer problems such as not getting the number of a person who can solve the problem or of the decision maker.

Sending poor quality or resealed cartons or boxes or selling articles outside the expiry date or, worse of all, selling fakes.

What do companies need to do to prevent this kind of Customer Value Starvation?

Ideas to Prevent Value Starvation

The customer thinking has put the pursuit of delight ahead of the pursuit of ending misery. This thinking also emanates from the imagination that hunting is more prestigious than farming. Taking care of customers is secondary to getting new customers.

The real customer misery (read Customer Value Starvation) experience comes when companies believe that they can throw their responsibilities onto the customer.

If you buy something new, you expect it to work. If it doesn't, you expect the company will take care of making it work. The company throws this task onto your lap. This happens whether it is the primary company making the product or the secondary selling the product; they all seem to be saying, a faulty product is your problem. We got it to you, now you get it to us, and wait. Instead of saying, we understand you bought the product to fulfil a need (an ink cartridge to keep my printer running, a cell phone so that I can make calls, and so on), the company is saying I do not care about your need. You just don't print for a few days or do not make calls for a few days. There is no replacement, only repair. And you have to spend your time to get it to us or to our store. That is no longer our headache. Our responsibility ended when we delivered the faulty product.

And often, the problem could be minor. It could even be that the instructions are not there to help the customer understand how to get rid of the problem.

Companies do not realize the serious cost to them and the customer of all this. The time and effort on either side is enormous.

Most customers for most things do not need an experience. They want everything to work. Concentrate on this and not on experience.

Experience is simply the name we give our mistakes.
...Oscar Wilde
So if companies make no mistake, is it a good experience?

The time has come for zero defects and zero complaints. Why are these complaints occurring? How do we prevent them (for example, repackaged returned goods from being sent out by a company's reseller;

common complaints like I cannot hear on the phone for a brand new phone, by suggesting on the plastic protector, "Remove before use," and so on)?

Why are companies happy about killing customers? Don't they see that the death of customers will also kill them?

When Zero Defects Are the Norm, Why Not Zero Customer Complaints?

There was a time when there was no such phrase like *zero defects*. It was accepted that some defects would always remain. But management gurus like Dr. Joseph Juran and W. Edwards Demming convinced management that zero defects were not only possible but could also create a competitive advantage.

Today, it is accepted that customer service is necessary, and good customer service creates a competitive advantage. Unfortunately, customer service efficiency is measured by customer satisfaction that measure transactions and not embedded feelings over a period of time, which is quantifiable by measuring customer value. Another measure is complaints per thousand interactions. Many companies are happy to have 10 or less complaints per 1,000, or 1 percent. Some companies achieve 0.1 percent complaints. And they rest on their laurels.

Whenever a complaint gets escalated upward to management, the general thought is to solve the complaint (and not always to the customer's satisfaction).

Few think about systemic means to change processes and old, set procedures.

Much of this happens because the job of managers is to solve the problem. They do not or are not asked to reach zero customer complaints. If they were to look at the problem from this viewpoint, not only would the problem be solved, but the complaint or customer problem would also not occur in the future.

I just bought overseas travel insurance on the internet. Unfortunately, I had to extend the duration of the insurance which was due to start a month from this time. To extend the policy, I got on the phone and found one number on the company's website but this number did not exist. A second number was difficult to get to and when I would get through, I was made to answer many questions and listen to many unnecessary ads. I would be put on hold for the next available agent. And then I would get disconnected. I had to go through a few iterations before I got to talk to an agent. No, the policy could not be extended (he did not know how). The best would be for me to cancel the policy and get a new one for a longer time period. So I requested cancellation. The agent could not tell me when I would get my refund. Almost 20 days later, I managed (through influence) to get the number of a senior executive. He was very apologetic. A few days later, I still did not have the refund. So I sent an e-mail again. This time an executive working for the company called me because his boss had asked him to help me get a refund. I had to fill a form for a refund. I told him I had not filled any form for getting the policy, and why now, and why the call center had not told me about the form. To cut a long story short, he said he would arrange for a refund. The executives would never go back and get the problems corrected using software, processes, and procedures so that others would not have a problem, which would lead to zero customer complaints.

Larry Malarkar, the loyalty expert and an experienced hotelier, suggests that the metric should not only be the number of complaints but also the number of iterations to solve a complaint.

> Companies need to embrace the concept of zero customer complaints and work on reducing problems for customers. What a different customer experience zero customer complaints would be!

—Adapted from a Gautam Mahajan Article

Reflections on Customer Value Starvation

by Shep Hyken

This chapter is written by Customer Service Expert Shep Hyken for this book. Shep gives examples of Customer Value Starvation and how to overcome them. Adapted from: https://www.forbes.com/sites/ shephyken/2018/05/10/starbucks-gets-an-a-in-crisis-management

Sometimes things don't go right. Sometimes there are mistakes and problems. They may be our fault or not. Regardless of what happens, every negative situation is an opportunity to learn.

For example, a while back I had dinner at a favorite restaurant. Unfortunately, a bad customer service experience tainted the evening. The good news is that this event created a learning opportunity.

By the way, you don't have to be in the restaurant business to appreciate and learn from this story. As I take you through the story and the lessons we can take away from it, think about how they apply to your business.

On that evening I ordered the pasta dish that I've been ordering for years. It came out wrong. It had peas in it. Not just a few peas, but loaded with peas. And I hate peas. I picked up the menu and confirmed that I hadn't misread the description. Nowhere did it say peas. I motioned the server over and told her about the problem. She had a great attitude and was happily going to take care of the situation. But, just about then, the manager who had been observing, stepped in. I had never seen this manager before. He didn't apologize and instead told me that they have two chefs and that this one likes to put peas in the pasta dishes. He said that most people find that the peas are a pleasant surprise.

Ah, that explains it. A pleasant surprise—not for me! And I nicely told him so. He just stared at me. I could tell how uncomfortable the server was at this interaction. She wanted to do something, but the manager had taken over, and he was blowing it.

Eventually, the manager asked if I would like to get a different pasta entree. I asked if they could make the same dish without the peas, as was on the menu. He finally took the dish away.

Several lessons come out of this incident:

1. The server was handling things just fine. The manager got in the way of her taking care of me. The manager didn't respond with the same enthusiastic attitude of taking care of me, the way the server did. He didn't even apologize. Managers should set examples— good examples.
2. The manager should have immediately taken the dish away. If you can get a problem out of the customer's sight, do it quickly. Once the dish has been taken away, then launch into recovery mode.
3. The manager made an excuse rather than giving an explanation. There is a fine line between excuses and explanations. An explanation comes with an apology and doesn't come across as defensive or aggressive.
4. The manager wasn't listening to me. Why would he call the peas a pleasant surprise when he knew I didn't want them in the pasta? Because, he was defending the decision of his chef to change the ingredients. (Read that as changing a process if you aren't in the restaurant business.)

Finally, the incident broke the consistency of prior experiences, which now leads to a lack of confidence. The next time I order this pasta dish I'm going to have to ask if it has peas, because you never know who's cooking in the back. Will it be the chef who likes to "pleasantly surprise" people with ingredients that aren't listed on the menu or the chef who follows the recipes I love—the ones that make me want to come back again and again.

The restaurant is great, and I'm going back, because I know this is an isolated incident. But what if this was my first or second time at this restaurant? Given all of the good places there are to eat, would I want to spend my hard-earned money at a restaurant, or with any type of business, that makes mistakes? My friend Tom Baldwin, former CEO of Morton's Steakhouse, says, "Great service is mistakes handled well." That's great advice for any business.

So, how do you handle mistakes well? And, sometimes it's not a mistake, but a problem. And, sometimes that problem is even our fault.

As an example, the airlines are prone to delayed and cancelled flights. Often, they are due to circumstances beyond the airline's control. It wasn't that long ago that United Airlines had a computer outage that lasted two and a half hours and caused 200 flight delays and six cancellations. Keep in mind, there wasn't just one unhappy customer complaining to a gate agent at the airport about a delayed flight. This situation involved thousands of people who were inconvenienced.

I would describe a 2-plus-hour delayed flight as a Moment of Misery™.

There were thousands of angry passengers. Yet, problems like this are bound to happen at some point; just last year it happened with Delta and Southwest. And it may not be a computer glitch, but a weather problem that causes airline delays. Yet every cloud has a silver lining, and in this instance it's a mini case study on how to handle a customer service crisis.

I can't speak to what happened at the airport when passengers approached gate agents for help, or what happened on the phone lines as passengers tried to reach a customer service representative. I'm sure there were long lines and hold times. The individual interactions turned out either good or bad because of the individual employees' attitudes and how well they have been trained to handle such situations. But, what I can speak to is the general response that United Airlines made, and how it was a perfect example of what to do in a crisis situation.

I teach a five-step process to deal with a complaining customer, and for those who follow my work, this is a short review:

1. Acknowledge the problem.
2. Apologize for the problem.
3. Fix the problem—or discuss how it will be fixed.
4. Do it with the right attitude—not just being nice, but acting accountable.
5. Doing all of this with a sense of urgency.

Well, the same way you deal with individual customers is also the way you deal with a customer service crisis that impacts thousands of customers.

First, United acknowledged and apologized for the inconvenience. That's steps one and two. They responded to media inquiries and tweeted out to all of their followers: A ground stop is in place for domestic flights due to an IT issue. We're working on a resolution. We apologize for the inconvenience.

Then they fixed it, accomplishing step three.

Step four was that they accepted responsibility. Maddie King, a spokesperson for United, met with the press and told them they were working to fix the problem. No excuses. In other words, United owned the problem.

Finally, there was a sense of urgency behind all of this. It took just two and a half hours to fix the problem. They worked hard and fast. Urgency is key to restoring confidence.

So, be it an individual complaining or a major customer service crisis affecting thousands of customers, consider the five-step process that not only fixes what is broken, but potentially restores the customer's confidence. And, done well it may restore the customer's confidence to a level higher than if the problem had never happened at all.

Here's another example from a completely different industry. Using that same five-step process, a company turned that complaint, or as I call it, a Moment of Misery™, into what I call a Moment of Magic.

Intuit, the company that created TurboTax software for individuals to do their own taxes, made a customer service mistake. The good news is that they turned it around and thereby created a great case study for us to learn from.

Here is the short version: In the most recent update of their software, the developers of TurboTax purposely left out a very important feature that had been included in earlier versions. Certain customers who had used TurboTax for years found out in the middle of doing their tax preparation that they would have to pay more to get an upgrade that included the necessary forms for them to complete their return.

The customers affected by the change were upset. So upset that they went on Amazon.com and other review sites and gave TurboTax a one-star rating.

So, how did Intuit react to the uproar?

The first thing they did was apologize. On the Intuit website, which sells TurboTax, an apology was made and an offer to refund $25 to customers who paid extra to file their tax returns. Sason Goodarzi, general manager of TurboTax, made the following statement:

> We messed up. We made a change this year to TurboTax desktop software and we didn't do enough to communicate this change to you as proactively and broadly as we could or should have. I am very sorry for the anger and frustration we may have caused you.

Apparently this wasn't enough. Shortly after the apology on the website, Intuit's CEO, Brad Smith, posted a video on his LinkedIn account that included the following message: "We're taking new steps to make things right." Smith's heartfelt apology helped.

Intuit had a crisis on their hands. The customer reaction was anger and a loss of loyalty, as customers switched to Intuit's competition, H & R Block. The mistake was that they made a change to a product that some say put profit motive ahead of their customer. Nothing wrong with making a profit, but how you go about it is very important.

So, Intuit had to make a quick move. They did some things right to bring back many of their customers. If you look at their reaction, they used the five-step process we covered earlier in this chapter:

1. They acknowledged the problem as they saw the customer comments.
2. They apologized for it. Very important, whenever there is a mistake. This mistake was big enough that the CEO had to make a public apology, which sent a very positive message.
3. They fixed the problem by offering the refunds and upgrades.
4. They took accountability. The general manager and the CEO's message was clear that they were taking steps to right the wrong.
5. They did it quickly. Their fast reaction convinced many of the customers who were thinking of abandoning the software to stay.

Is it enough? I'm sure that some customers won't come back; yet, many will. The way the problem was handled proved that Intuit listens to their customers. Intuit learned a valuable lesson, and by the way they handled it, so did we. The five steps mentioned are exactly how most situations should be handled to not just fix the problem, but to also restore the customer's confidence.

There's one more example I'd like to share. This isn't about a customer complaint. This is a full-blown crisis. Once again, using the five-step process, a major crisis was managed in a way that turned a PR nightmare into an opportunity to prove to the public how good this company really is.

Starbucks has become a brand recognized throughout the world and is recognized for the quality experience they create for their customers with some of the best coffee and best customer service. Some of you reading may be familiar with the racial bias incident that occurred in a Starbucks in Philadelphia. I was impressed with the speed at which Starbucks stepped up to apologize and accept responsibility for the incident in which two innocent customers were arrested while waiting for a friend.

There is no doubt racism is a touchy subject. My opinion is that Starbucks handled this well. There are a few naysayers out there who disagree. Some felt Starbucks could have done more. Some felt they did what they did just to save face. Some even thought the company capitalized on the experience and turned it into a PR opportunity. Here's my take. Starbucks had to do something, and it had to be done fast. As mentioned, I felt Starbucks handled the situation well, so well that I'm sharing what I think is the perfect example of how to manage a brand crisis.

Here is the short version of the story. Two black gentlemen were waiting for a friend and didn't want to order anything until he showed up. Because they were just sitting in the store and hadn't bought anything (yet), the manager asked them to leave. When they didn't, the manager called the police. The men were arrested and held for hours before they were released without being charged.

The incident went public, and as some would say, viral. Immediately, Starbucks leadership stepped up. Howard Schultz, chairman of Starbucks, said, "I'm embarrassed, ashamed. I think what occurred was reprehensible at every single level. I take it very personally, as everyone in our company does, and we're committed to making it right."

In addition to Schultz's apology, Starbucks announced that it would be closing more than 8,000 stores in just a couple of months to conduct racial bias training for 175,000 employees. Schultz said, "It will cost millions of dollars, but I've always viewed this and things like this as not an expense, but an investment in our people and our company. And we're better than this."

So, let's break this down. Once again, the five-step process is at work.

1. The first thing that Starbucks did was acknowledge the problem. The executives didn't hunker down with attorneys for several days before coming out with a statement. It was quick. The highest ranking officer, the chairman, went on national TV with his comments. Schultz wasn't defensive. On the contrary, he was very decisive about the action they would take.

2. Starbucks acknowledged the problem. Schultz's statement was quick and to the point. He used words such as embarrassed and ashamed, which everyone could relate to. He also said, "We're better than this."

3. Starbucks issued an apology. Schultz's actions were swift and sincere.

4. Starbucks shared its solution, which would start with the closing of thousands of stores for racial bias training. Whether this is the right solution or not, it showed Starbucks was committed to making things right.

5. Starbucks owned what happened. Its leadership held nothing back in their comments about how unhappy they were with what happened. The concept of *owning a problem* is not always easy. People make excuses or become defensive. Nowhere in this process was there a deflection of what happened.

6. Starbucks leadership acted with urgency. This could have gone out of control, but the speed in which they acted showed the importance they were placing on the incident.

This is textbook crisis management. If you want to go through an interesting exercise, just Google "biggest brand crises" or "public relations disasters," and read the stories of how companies handled their problems. There have been PR disasters as a result of poor judgment from employees, data breaches that impacted millions of consumers, and more. You'll find good examples, and unfortunately, bad examples to learn from. But, if you want the textbook perfect way to handle a crisis, look no further than the excellence demonstrated by Starbucks. It raised the bar on how to do what's right when something goes wrong.

Another interesting article by Shep Hyken, with his permission https:// hyken.com/customer-service-3/the-boss-can-kill-the-customer-service-buzz/. We couldn't resist putting it in.

The Boss Can Kill the Customer Service Buzz

"Don't let the boss kill the customer service buzz!"

Taken from https://hyken.com/customer-service-3/the-boss-can-kill-the-customer-service-buzz/ with permission

Back in my high school and college days I worked at a gas station. We were a self-service station, so our role was that of cashier more than anything else.

One very cold morning I noticed an elderly woman drive into the station. She was probably 80 years old. When I say it was a cold morning, I mean it was record-breaking cold.

I walked out to her car and asked if I could fill her tank with gas for her so she could stay in her warm car. She was happy to stay warm and I was happy to help her. Once her tank was full, she paid me, I thanked her, and she drove off.

I hustled back into the warm building where my manager asked, "What did you just do?"

I thought it was a strange question since it was obvious, but I said, "I filled that woman's car with gas."

He said, "Son, this is a self-service gas station. Now she's going to expect that the next time she comes back." I responded by saying, "I hope she does come back instead of going to the station across the street or the one on the opposite corner." He gave me an angry look and walked away.

I was young, but I wasn't stupid. Simply put, it was the right thing to do. If she came back on another cold day, I would do it again.

There are two big lessons here. First, we all have two responsibilities: do the job we were hired to do and also take care of the customer. I may have been a cashier, but I also knew that my job, beyond collecting money, was to take care of my customers.

Second, a boss can kill the customer service buzz. I believed in taking care of my customers so strongly that my boss couldn't, even with his anger and negativity, change my mind about this. Unfortunately, if my boss talked that way to most of the other employees I worked with, they would be scared to death to go out on the drive and help a customer.

Quite often, if a company is considered a customer service laggard, it is because of its leadership and management. One of the most important ways a leader can foster a customer-focused culture is by modeling that behavior—in other words, by treating employees how they want the customer treated. In addition, leadership must empower good employees to take care of the customer the best way they see fit. If it's wrong, coach them on how to do it right. If it's right, coach them to do more of the same. No matter what, don't kill the customer service buzz!

Shep Hyken is a customer service expert, keynote speaker, and New York Times bestselling business author. For information, contact 314-692-2200 or www.hyken.com. For information on The Customer Focus™ customer service training programs go to www.thecustomerfocus.com. Follow on Twitter: @ Hyken (Copyright © MMXX, Shep Hyken)

Shep shows us that Customer Value Starvation can be prevented by creating a total company culture that is customer friendly. It is like a mountain stream that flows from the top down and into the lake, as in Costco and Starbucks. Unfortunately, in many companies, Customer Value Starvation is addressed to a less effective extent, by customer friendly individuals, who are like an oasis in the desert, working (in spite of discouragement from bosses) to remain customer friendly and create loyalty.

Are Assumptions Hurting Your Brand?

by V. N. Bhattacharya

V. N. Bhattacharya is Adjunct Professor, IIM Bangalore, and Independent Consultant Business and Corporate Strategy

I was enjoying lunch with friends on a pleasant December afternoon, when my phone rang. The caller, an ICICI Bank Card representative, asked if I had paid the bill that had fallen due a few days ago. I apologized and said how sorry I was that I had forgotten to. I assured the young man I would pay it in full the same day. I did. It had so happened that I had also forgotten to pay Citibank Card bills for the same period. I paid them too.

The same evening I wrote to ICICI Bank. I reiterated that it had slipped from my mind and requested them to reverse late payment penalty and interest charges they might levy. I cited our long relationship and my impeccable track record of payment (both true). I wrote an identical mail to Citibank, first for waiver of penalty and later for reversal of interest charges (a much larger sum!).

In the next 2 days I received four phone calls from ICICI Bank repeatedly asking if I had made the payment.

Unconvinced when I said I had, they asked for payment reference. I also received a call in which a recorded voice informed me my card had been blocked. Thank you very much!

Guilty Till Proven Innocent?

ICICI Bank promptly responded with a refusal to my request for waiver of penalty and interest with this e-mail:

> We value your relationship with ICICI Bank. However, based on the bank's policy, we regret to inform you that we are unable to

reverse the charges levied on your credit card. We thank you for giving us an opportunity to be of service to you.

They also sent me a message saying the overdue payment is affecting my credit history with CIBIL and that it may prevent me from getting a loan or credit card from any bank in future. An indirect threat? I wondered why they were giving me so much grief for having delayed payment of just Rs 6,817.04 by only 6 days.

I wrote to ICICI Bank's Head of Credit Policy and Processes requesting him to intervene. When I did not receive any reply I wrote to another senior manager with whom I had been acquainted briefly a few years ago. I also sent them reminders. Neither of them acknowledged any of my mails.

Citibank, on the other hand, responded in 24 hours, first reversing penalties for late payment and later interest charges. No fuss.

Spot the Difference

I have speculated why there would be such a *stark difference* in the behavior of two banks competing pretty much in the same space for similar segments of customers. Presumably ICICI Bank wants to retain credit-worthy customers who spend regularly. That is why I suspect they had given me a credit limit of Rs 100,000.

It seems reasonable to assume they would wish to avoid undue risk of defaulters. But does one error—*honestly confessed*—make a customer a credit risk? So much so that they have to call him four times and not so subtly threaten him? Incidentally, ICICI Bank blocked my card *without warning* when the payment was due. They unblocked it 10 days later, when I wrote to them.

Actions of employees are driven by policies. What policies drove/drive ICICI Bank's actions? Perhaps they believe defaulters must be dealt with an iron hand lest they become delinquent?

A Question of Assumptions

Our decisions are quietly shaped by assumptions. Often they remain unarticulated. Unarticulated beliefs stay unchallenged. Surreptitiously they influence policies and guide employee behavior. Occasionally, they border on the mindless, hurt customer goodwill and the firm's reputation.

Could senior managers strive to make assumptions explicit and question them from time to time? Or, should they let policies rule? They would do well to remember customers do not become advocates when a firm does everything right. They become staunchly loyal when firms surprise them with a kind and generous gesture.

I did eventually get an e-mail from ICICI Bank (17 days after my first request) waiving off the late fee and interest charge. Couldn't the bank have done it sooner, *graciously?*

Building a Customer-Centric Organization

by B. S. Nagesh

Moving from Customer Value Starvation to Customer Value Creation

B. S. Nagesh is Chairman of Retailers Association of India; Founder, TRRAIN; Nonexecutive Chairman, Shoppers Stop Ltd.

The twenty-first century has put tremendous power in the hands of the customer. She can, at the click of a button, shop anytime during the day or night; she can recommend you, your brand, and your company to a group of friends whereas at the same time she can bring you down. Internet, social media, and digital platforms have made her more knowledgeable than people working in the company. In most cases she is more educated than the person serving her and is more informed about the product than people behind the brand.

The environment and the markets have become very competitive and the disruptions have a tremendous impact on multiple industries. Most disruptions are from outside the incumbent industry. Brands and companies that are inward looking and do not have an outside-in perspective are losing grounds.

In such environments we see brands getting wiped out because they did not create value for the customer at multiple levels. Some of the touch points that lead to Customer Value Starvation are as follows:

- The retail environment: Brands have to ensure that the store they are present in is aligned to their target segment and their likes and dislikes.
- If it is a retail brand selling through an exclusive brand store, then the store layout, furniture, fixtures have to be fully aligned to the brand promise.

- Presentation and visual displays are critical to enhancing the customer experience.
- Last mile customer service delivery always happens by the associate, whether a sales, service, or delivery associate. Hence, an untrained, not presentable associate with little knowledge and poor conversational skills lets a brand down and starves the customer from getting value out of the brand and of course the product, and the brand promise is also not delivered.

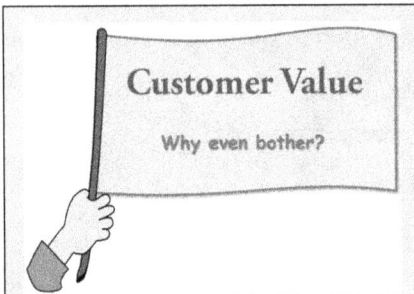

Customer Value

Why even bother?

Why is the most important business concept so unpopular?

Most people agree that customer value is probably the most important business concept of all. It is the very foundation for the existence of any business and organization.
On LinkedIn:

- 393 people follow the hashtag #customervalue
- 42,563 people follow the hashtag #customerexperience
- 38,117,847 people follow the hashtag #innovation

The numbers are, to say the least, startling. A way to demonstrate this is to make the following analogy if we all were medical doctors instead:

- Inadequate features and poor-quality product can also lead to business failures.
- Dysfunctional organization with functions working in Silos.

In India we have seen Customer Value Starvation in a big way in the restaurant business.

In one of the conferences I was told that 80 percent of restaurants in India close within 30 months. When you look back and try to find the reasons, it's always one or all of the aforementioned. In addition to these, poor skill sets and managerial capabilities lead to such Starvation. Every good cook cannot become a successful food service entrepreneur. One has to be passionate and has to have the skill sets to run the business.

India has had many clo-sures in the retail business. Two big, largely funded companies that went bust in the early 2000s were Subhiksha, in the food business, funded by private equity investors and Koutons, in the apparel business, publicly funded through the equity markets. When we look back, one realizes that the organizational purpose was also flawed and not aligned to delivering customer value. Both the companies had first-time entrepreneurs. The organizations were built with the objective of creating capacity and growth at any cost, losing sight of customers. While chasing growth they were only concentrating on opening stores and filling them with merchandise.

One of the biggest flaws I have seen that leads to Customer Value Starvation is when brands think short term and are chasing to create transactional values rather than having a long-term view of building a relationship

- 393 doctors are interested in learning how to *diagnose diseases better*
- 42,563 are interested in *stress management*
- 38,117,847 think *heart transplantations* are the thing patients need

Customer experience and innovation will fail if it doesn't rest on a companywide understanding of customer value. Shar VanBoskirk framed it in an excellent way:

"Most firms have no clear definition of 'value.' Not having a clear, shared definition of value prevents an organization from rallying stakeholders around the concept."

Customer value is defined in the European standard EN 12973. Numerous people, including myself, have expanded the standard and transformed it into concrete and practical tools to guide an organization to success.

Why are so few people interested? Asks Per Lindstedt, 8-Step-VoC / Value Model Founder

with the customer and looking at creating an opportunity to capture life time value (LTV) of the customer. One needs to learn this concept from Indian jewelers who serve generations of customers by building trust and ensure getting reference, strong word of mouth, and endorsement from family members. They make us rethink the LTV of a customer to LTV of families and generations.

Another lost opportunity is seen in the automobile industry where although the customer is tied in for 5 to 10 years the industry does not look at building a great relationship with their customers other than the transaction. I have personally experienced this issue. I had a Honda CRV car that was 10 years old. The car was going to the same service station for all these years. From the 11th year it started giving trouble and had to be sent to the garage almost every few months. Promptly after the service I would get a call on service feedback. But the service organization never spoke to the sales organization informing them to meet me to help me get a new car so that they could replace my car with a new version of their brand. It never happened and I finally bought a different brand of car. Service function was chasing service revenue and sales function was concerned with chasing new customers.

Similar golden opportunities lie in the electronics and durables industry. This is the only business where the service technician gets an entry into every room of the customer's house, including personal spaces, whether it is to service kitchen appliances, air conditioners, or tucked away lockers in corners of the bedroom. He gets to interact with the customer in their comfortable home environment. If trained well, they can become the eyes and ears of the business and can suggest and sell much more than anyone in the core sales team. The only need is for both the sale and service team to work together and all the functions having a common objective to satisfy the customers when they are using the product.

The above examples lead us to think on how one can build a customer-centric organization. My experience says that the customer value creation should be built in the purpose of the organization. Everyone, whether in the store or in the HO, has to think customer first. Every individual's key result area (KRA) should have 20 to 25 percent key performance indicators (KPIs) around the customer, and the customer should be the center of every decision-making. Talking to customers and meeting the ultimate consumers on a regular basis should be mandated.

Let's not forget, these are our expectations when we as customers want to buy or use a service.

Gautam's comments: We instituted Customer Centric Circles at the front line at Godrej. The ensuing result was great interaction between service and sales teams, leading to a 30-percent increase in sales a month after the program was launched.

Walter's comments: There are many examples of deficiency in retail leading to Customer Value Starvation. Here are a few examples.

Value Starvation in Retail

Paytm Mall/Apple

Gautam bought an Apple cell phone via Paytm on the 10th. It did not work. On the 11th he called and after an hour was told it could only be picked up and not replaced or canceled. On the 16th, he had an e-mail on the 14th as follows:

Dear Gautam,

I understand that you are facing issues with Apple iPhone 7 32 GB Black with order number _____. To help us resolve your query faster, we request you provide us a service job sheet. To arrange the job sheet you can contact the brand customer care number at 000-800-100-9009, and schedule a free visit by brand service engineer or you can also visit the nearest brand service centre.

And so on with other delaying tactics!

Walter comments: As if this was not enough, we have reports that consumers are cheated at every step. Ironically, even weights and measures, weighing scales and measuring tapes are often fake and tampered.

Consumers cheated at each step, reveals weights and measures

Consumers and activists are always surprised to learn the myriad ways in which they are cheated with every purchase, be it real estate, mobile recharge vouchers, fuel, or packaged or unpackaged food.

Other sources reveal some petrol pumps often dispense lesser quantities than what motorists pay for, especially if people buy less than 5 liters.

Already, real estate firms are wary of the department's move to measure flats and ensure that buyers get what was promised. Builders say our inspectors are equipped to weigh only potatoes and tomatoes, that we will not understand the technicalities of property deals. Fortunately, the state government is supportive of our campaign. Ironically, even weights and measures, weighing scales and measuring tapes are often fake or tampered.

Does business mean only cheating or starving the consumer?

Walter's musings

You remember Philip Kotler said, "The more successful a company becomes, the faster it forgets the very lessons that made it successful." It would seem obvious. One would have thought that all companies know this. Perhaps, they do. But in their change of focus from Customer to Wall Street, or any other concerns, they forget who is at the source of their business—and, in many ways, their success.

This happens with big companies and small businesses. The business grows. The organizational structure builds up into a pyramid. Those who founded the business are now at the top of the pyramid, and isolated from those below, living in their own rarefied atmospheres. Those at the bottom of the pyramid have little commitment to the job, to the company, or to the customer. The result can only be described through a story briefed in the next article on Walgreen.

Below is a hierarchy of destroying and advocacy clusters. Our aim is to create long-term value. Destructive clusters start as Customer Value Starvation clusters.

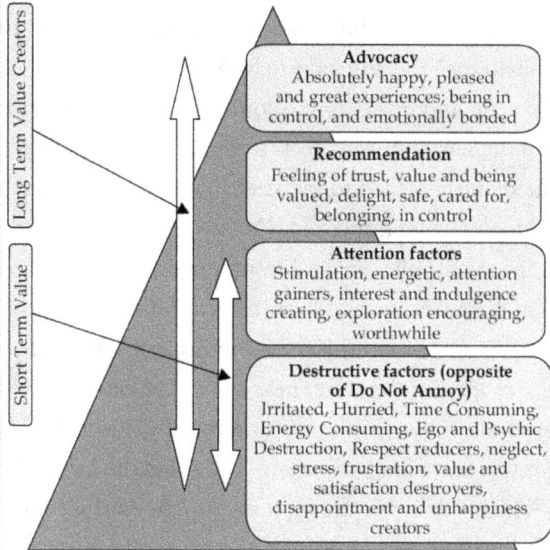

Source: Author Gautam Mahajan

At Walgreens

A visitor from Ireland, who owned a chain of supermarkets there, was visiting Chicago. I met him at the business school in Chicago and we began exchanging thought on customer care. He seemed very disappointed with the levels of customer care in the United States. Why? I asked him. He said that he had gone to Walgreens, the chemist chain shop, because he wanted to buy an analgesic. Outside the store was a big poster: "SMILE AT CUSTOMERS WEEK." He went to the pharmacist who suggested the product, then went to the cashier to pay. Then went to the collection counter to collect the parcel—and found all of them without a hint of a smile.

Finally, he asked the girl at the delivery counter, "Why is everyone frowning here? I thought this is smile at Customers week." Prompt came the reply, "Oh! That was last week! Thank God it's over."

As Larry Malarkar would say, you cannot avoid Customer Value Starvation by mandate!

At Marks & Spencer

I went to Marks & Spencer in London—one of their branches near Bond Street—to buy thermal underwear for a trip to a cold country. Asked one of the saleswomen passing by for directions, who very casually said I could try the first floor. I did. It was a huge hall, with various sections. Can anyone help me? You will have to look around, they said. I wandered around quite a lot, and finally found some racks with thermal underwear. I picked up four sets and went to the counter. Before I pay, can I have these measured and matched to my size? I don't want to make a mistake. The assistant took one look and said, "No need. It is size 14. I don't need a measuring tape to tell you." I paid. I went home and tried it on. It was one size too large. The assistant had been overconfident and cocky. The customer is irritated by this and this irritation is Customer Value Starvation.

When I was leaving the store, near the exit, I was confused. Was the underground train station at the left or right of the exit? I had forgotten, but I knew it was just a few yards away. So I asked the lady assistant at the exit lobby. Which side is it—the right or the left? And she answered with a brusque "I don't know"!

This is also a case of unhelpfulness that is seen by the customer as Customer Value Starvation.

So while M&S were busy overhauling the business, because they were losing their share of the market, and refurbishing stores and amending product lines, their employees were busy losing customers, many of whom vowed not to return again.

Again, the distance between the top management and the bottom of the pyramid had grown so large that there was no connect. Sadly, Customer Value Starvation had come to stay, which would finally ruin the company and top management would never know why. This is because they feel they have done the best for the company with product selection, shop decor, reasonable pricing, and sufficient advertising and promotion. Yet, why are they not succeeding?

Because the more successful a company becomes, the greater the distance between the top management and the final customer:

And top management is inclined to forget the very lessons that made the company successful.

Examples of Customer Value Starvation

The Good (Customer Value Creation) and the Ugly (Customer Value Starvation)

Here are good and bad experiences we have had with various companies and segments of business and government. These are meant to give the reader ideas about value starvers and value creators.

Restaurants

Walter's Experience

I have some experiences with restaurants, as I am sure most of us do—at least those of us who live in large towns, and go out a lot to eat.

About 40 years ago, my wife and son went out to lunch at a restaurant in Bombay. They were very well known for their *biryani*—a rice preparation with chicken or lamb and spices that is

> Notice, Walter remembers Value Starvation and Value Creation even after 40 years.
> Do not cause value starvation, which is often long remembered.

slow cooked. We placed the order, and in the meantime, ordered some drinks till we were served. The plates were brought in about 15 minutes later, steaming hot. We had just about begun enjoying the food, when my son found a hair in the biryani.

Obviously, the cook had forgotten to wear his cap, at the time of cooking. We called the waiter and pointed this out to him. He did not seem shocked. Just took the plate away and then brought it back with the offending hair removed. Not even a word of apology.

And the gall to bring the same dish back, with the suggestion that now you can go ahead and enjoy it. None of us could bring ourselves to finish the meal. We paid the bill. Did not leave a tip—and left. We never visited this restaurant again. As my son always joked: We did not want to be lucky again!

The Customer is looking for the waiter to point out a dead fly on his bubbling fresh lime soda. As the bubbles broke, the fly seemed to be dancing. "There is a fly dancing on my fresh lime soda," snarled the irritated customer.

For Rs 40, what do you expect, Marilyn Monroe to be dancing, asked the waiter, cool and smiling

This was an example of Customer Value Starvation and now here is an example of Customer Value Creation. My wife and I were with our son in San Jose, California, 5 years ago. We went to dinner at a restaurant in the town center. It was highly rated for the quality of food and ambience.

And once again, we were *lucky*. My wife found a hair in her dish. We called the waiter and showed him what we were complaining about. He immediately called the manager. The latter was very apologetic. He took the dish away. Asked my wife if she could choose something else. She did.

When we finished the meal, the bill folder was given to me. There was no bill. The restaurant waived the total bill. There was a letter of apology. And there was a voucher for a meal (with a limit) for the next visit to the restaurant.

Two different ways of handling the same problem. The real solution, even if the occurrences are two continents apart, is to improve systems and have regular checks, whatever you may produce and sell. Take all complaints with the seriousness they deserve. Get senior management involved and let them show that they are involved. Make the customer feel the emotive connect. It will show that any deficiency hurts you as much as it hurts him.

Many times it works to use prevention rather than cure of Customer Starvation in restaurants.

"Anything to drink, sir?" "No, nothing. Just water." After a while, the water is brought, but also a small glass of fruit juice—"It's on the house."

Before taking the plates away, "Some dessert for you, sir?" "No, just get the bill." Before the bill is brought, there will be a small plate of chocolates or toffee served around—"With the compliments of the house."

After all this, of course, you will go there again!

I was having lunch at my club some time ago and was relating the U.S. restaurant story to my friend, who responded with a reluctant appreciation of how the restaurant had acted, but added that in the United States, the restaurant would have to pay a heavy price if the customer had sued them for *this carelessness*. Yes, this was perhaps also a good reason: a sword having over their heads.

It reminded me of a restaurant I revisited in Singapore and was shocked to find it closed. What happened? The notice said, "Closed for 3 months," because (I later discovered) the food inspector on a regular check found the kitchen below expected hygiene standards. This is so unlike our roadside stalls in Mumbai, which wash plates in dirty water and reuse them to serve the steady stream of new customers, who are not greatly disturbed by what they see—questionable hygiene standards like the dirty food cart, the polluted air, the pail of water for rewashing, service without gloves, and the clothes worn by the serving staff that were once white. All this Customer Value Starvation does not seem to affect business.

Gautam's comments: It also could be that customers do not notice the washing and so on and accept the unhygienic conditions.

Like most of you I have had experiences like the following with restaurants.

Many years ago, I was at the famous Oberoi Hotel in Delhi. I had invited a celebrity chef to the Oberoi's Chinese restaurant. The first dish was shark-fin soup. Both the celebrity and I were surprised at the lack of shark fins. We asked the waiter and he tried to prove there were adequate shark fins. Eventually, we asked for the chef, and he came and apologized that there were not adequate shark fins. He said he would replace the dish, which came back as it should be.

We were still unhappy at the waiter. After we finished lunch a delicious dessert arrived, and we were not billed for it. The captain had shifted a bad experience into a good one. Instead of Value Starvation there was Value Addition.

In Jordan, I entered a dessert café. It was busy and obviously popular. The desserts are mostly *halwa*, apart from the more known *baklava* and *kanafiyeh*.

After my wife and I sat down, I went to the counter to view the desserts. These were in huge platters, maybe 30 different types. People's orders were coming. The servings were huge. I did not know what to order. Obviously, I looked lost. The owner came to the counter and asked if he could help me. I said I did not know what to order and the servings were huge. He said, "Sir, why don't you sit down, and I will serve you." My wife was surprised I had not come back with a dessert. A few minutes later the owner brought me a plate with 12 samplings of different desserts. Smilingly, he said, "This is for you." Boy, was it delicious. After finishing we went to pay, and the owner said, "This is from us; no need to pay." How wonderful, and he had nothing to gain from us as potential repeat customers.

These are examples of giving with no expectation of a return. The unexpected gift, the best kind, and it is Customer Value Creation.

Hotels

It is nice to open the Customer Value Starvation section on hotels with a wonderful article by Denyse Drummond-Dunn.

How to Map Your Customer Journey and Overlay Their Emotions
by Denyse Drummond-Dunn

Denyse is President and Chief Catalyst of C3Centricity

With the travel and leisure industries in turmoil at the moment, now is a good time for them to review how they treat their customers. And mapping their customers' journey is an important step in understanding and satisfying the customer better.

Through the example of an experience I had with the Hilton Group, I share some important lessons about getting customer service right! These will be invaluable as countries start to open in the coming weeks and months.

Background

Each year around Christmas time, my family get together for a weekend of fun somewhere in Britain. This year we met up in Bristol. As a Hilton Honors member for more than 20 years I offered to book rooms for all of us in the local Doubletree. I expected to get a better rate with my membership, and especially cheaper than those offered by the booking sites. After all, why pay a booking site when I know the hotel I want to stay in, right? Well, I booked five rooms for the weekend, as well as a table for ten in their restaurant for dinner on Saturday evening.

I booked directly by calling the hotel, as I always prefer to do. I expected to be recognized for my loyalty, and if possible, rewarded too! On this occasion I was proven seriously wrong!

A couple of weeks after booking and prepaying for all the rooms, I received Hilton's weekly e-mail offering me a significant discount for the exact same hotel and dates. Clearly their online pixels had identified me as being interested in this hotel, but they hadn't connected this interest with my having booked directly. Already there, you can see that they have an incomplete customer journey mapping process.

As Hilton offer a "guaranteed lowest rate" I reached out to their call center and was told that yes, I was entitled not only to the lower rate, but to an additional 25 percent discount for having made the claim. I was told how to complete the claim form and I hung up ecstatic that I could save my family even more money, which we would no doubt anyway spend in the bar before and after our dinner!

Imagine my surprise when the next day I was told that my claim had been refused! I was informed that the guaranteed lowest rate only applied to third-party sites and not to Hilton's own website!

I immediately responded and was again told that their guarantee didn't apply to their own rates. In addition, as I had prepaid, I could not get the lower rate even if it was now being offered!

Not being one to take *no* for a final answer, I contacted their corporate customer service group again, as I felt my loyalty was not being recognized. I was once more given the same response, but this time was informed that my request would be forwarded directly to the hotel concerned, no doubt to get me off their (corporate) backs!

The hotel immediately responded saying that although it is corporate policy not to include direct bookings in their lowest rate guarantee, they would in this case give me the special offer. I was very pleased that they at least recognized the benefit of customer satisfaction and restored my faith in the Hilton Group, somewhat.

That should have been the end of this story, but it's not. Hilton have surpassed themselves this time in terms of customer service, or should I say a lack of it?

My brother called me the following week and informed me that the hotel's website was showing that their restaurant was closed on the day I had booked it. I immediately rang them and spoke to the same person, who remembered me and assured me our table for 10 people was booked. She said she would double-check just to be sure, so in the afternoon I called back not wanting any last-minute problems with my family.

Surprise, surprise, I was told the restaurant was booked for a private party. What about my reservation made more than a month ago? Shouldn't someone have contacted me? I demanded to speak to the manager, who apart from profuse apologies, said she would raise the issue in their operations meeting later that day.

She called me back that evening, to say that there was nothing she could do. It was their mistake and they would be happy to book me elsewhere in the city. I explained that my family had booked five rooms for two nights at their hotel so we could eat at their famous restaurant (my married sister had booked separately). No solution offered; an admission of fault but no compensation offered and no alternative other than to book at another restaurant! Their suggestion was their sister hotel down the road, a bland, modern affair, with no atmosphere.

This farcical situation continued during the whole weekend, but I won't bore you with the details, as I would rather use this incident to demonstrate how Hilton (and you) can be better prepared.

Three Lessons Learned That Every Business Can Apply

So what lessons are to be learned from this example, even if we work in a completely different industry? I came up with the following points but would love to hear what other issue of customer journey mapping you would add; just leave me a comment please.

1. **The customer journey map needs to integrate all possible contact points.**

   In Hilton's case this is clearly not done. I was personally offered a cheaper rate at the hotel at which I had already booked five rooms! Clearly they had identified that I had reviewed prices online and then offered me the cheaper rate.

Unfortunately, without their e-mail, I would never have known and would not have checked prices again since I had already booked. More importantly, I have now become dissatisfied with my booking, having been informed by Hilton that I could have paid less. Now I know that hotel prices can go up and down, but especially closer to the day of arrival. However, if this is not true (any longer) then I for one will only book last minute in future!

Lesson: You must include all touch points in your customer journey map, to avoid such disappointment. By using an incomplete model, Hilton opened themselves up to angering a loyal customer rather than appealing to potential new ones.

2. If you mess up, admit it *and* correct it.

After calling to book the rooms, the hotel put me through to the restaurant to book a table for the Saturday night. Everything was confirmed and I would not have checked details until arriving at the hotel and checking in.

The excuse that the closure of the restaurant is on their website didn't go down well with me when I called to check. After all, they themselves had taken the reservation *in person,* so why would I need to go to their website? It was anyway not possible to book the restaurant on their website!

Lesson: An apology for a mistake is not its resolution. Proposing to book another restaurant in their sister hotel was nothing more than I could have done myself. I didn't feel that Hilton were interested in correcting the situation that they themselves had created. They did not go out of their way to make things right. And I have had their loyalty card for decades!

When your company makes a mistake, find a solution that is acceptable to your customer, not just the quick fix that suits you. Now is your chance to not just satisfy, but to surprise and delight them.

3. Follow up to make sure the customer is happy.

I often speak about delighting the customer but your first aim is to ensure your customer is happy with the solution that you propose. Only after that can you look to see how you can go above and beyond what they expect, so they are both surprised and delighted with how they have been treated.

It takes a strong person to admit when they're wrong, but a stronger one to want to go beyond just putting it right. Which are you doing? Can you do more?

Lesson: Replacing a faulty product or service is what our customers expect. Offering free samples, a further discount, express delivery, or additional attention is not. These are the small touches that surprise and delight. They are also the things that your customers will share with friends and family, if not the whole world through social media. Suddenly, you have gone from being the bad guy to the cool guy.

Customer journey mapping has become much more complex today, as the touch points our customers are using, before, during, and after purchase, have expanded exponentially. However, the process of identifying and understanding the complete journey remains essential to delighting each and every customer.

One further element that I suggest my clients add to their journey maps is the emotional state of their customers at each interaction with a touch point. This simple addition is a powerful addition in clearly showing where a brand needs to improve its customers' interactions—it highlights those touch points where their customers' emotional experience is suboptimal and needs improving.

Gautam Mahajan's Recent Experience at Ramada Blue, Ahmedabad

We had made a confirmed booking for two rooms. We arrived at 11.30 p.m. (our expected time of arrival). The front desk person says he has to check if made-up rooms are available. After a few minutes, two rooms are given to us. I go to my room. It has still got housekeeping putting in fresh soap and so on. I ask them to turn the air conditioning on. It makes a racket. Housekeeping leaves.

Then I notice my bed has what looked like used sheets (not crisp, crumpled). The towels looked used. I call the front desk and tell him what happened. He says, wait, he is busy. Then after a few minutes, he says what is the problem after I had explained it to him! I re-explain, and he says housekeeping will come again. A housekeeping guy comes and says he is the supervisor. He agrees the sheets need changing. He goes across to the next room, pulls off the sheets from there, and installs in my room. I am too tired to argue. I cannot turn one light off as I cannot find the switch (why are hotels designed to make the customer look for things?). I turn off the main switch and finally fall asleep.

The next morning, in the other room my friend has, there is water flowing out from the shower area as the drain is clogged. The room is full of water.

In any event, there is damage control after I ask to speak to the general manager (I am not allowed to). I just wanted him to be aware and not to complain. No one allows me to contact him.

They change my room, to a new one, which is cleaned and then inspected by senior staff. This room is fine.

At breakfast, there are no napkins, no small spoons to stir the coffee, and my cappuccino comes with no spoon. How to stir the sugar in?

I wonder why all this happens. Is it lack of training? Is it lack of caring? How will they get a good name? This is Value Starvation at its worst. Larry Malarkar reminds me that if this continues to happen, than training is a solution.

Staff of China Star Hotels Cleans Toilet Seats, Cups with Same Cloth

Four or more major international hotel chains apologized recently after a hidden camera video of their room-cleaning practices in China was posted online.

The 11-minute video shows cleaners wiping cups and sinks with dirty towels and sponges. Some use the same towel to wipe the toilet seat.

The Shangri-La Hotel in Fuzhou said the actions in the video violate its standards, according to the *Times of India*.

And owners and top management can kill the golden goose that they created—through indiscretion and Customer Value Starvation.

Again, for the same reason, management of large five-star hotels can get complacent and not do adequate quality checks, thus creating Customer Value Starvation.

Airlines

Walter and Gautam have had varying interactions with airlines, both Customer Value Starvation and Customer Value Creation.

Emirates Airlines: A Good Customer Value Creation Experience

I(Walter) was traveling from Rome to Dubai and then, to Mumbai on March 28, 2019. I remembered I had used the iPad and sent out messages from the lounge at Rome airport. After that, I was blank about what happened. At Dubai airport, on arrival, I looked for the iPad in my hand baggage and it was not there. I must have left it in the lounge in Rome or in the seat pocket on the flight from Rome.

Since I had a few hours to change planes at Dubai airport, I filed a complaint. But the e-mail did not go through from my cell phone. When I got on the flight I explained my problem to the stewardess. She said she will help. When the plane is about 20,000 ft. above, one can use the internet. She took my mobile with the message to the purser when the internet worked. She confirmed she had sent the message. When I was home on March 29, I got a message asking me for a description of the iPad and the code. A few hours later, they confirmed Emirates was sending the iPad through a purser on the Dubai–Mumbai evening flight, and could I collect it from Mumbai Airport on March 30 anytime during the day? I did. It was all so smooth, pleasant and courteous. I think I have become an Emirates fan now.

The Ugly (Customer Value Starvation) Experience in the Airline World

Dear Swati,

We had booked a ticket through your Company, Velocity Travels, and on your recommendation, from Mumbai to San Jose in California, USA, for July 18, 2018, 01.45 hours by British Airlines.

Even though it meant some hours wait at London, we made this choice because our son was to receive us in San Jose, where he lives. We therefore did not take the option of flying to San Francisco, and then driving to San Jose.

However, when we arrived at Mumbai airport, to check in at 12 midnight (after net check in), we were told that the flight from London to San Jose is canceled, because of problems at Dallas airport for the past few days, which has upset airline schedules everywhere!

They kindly offered to accommodate my wife (71 years) and get her a seat on a flight to San Francisco, through Seattle and somewhere else, and to accommodate me (79) years on another flight which will be on another route. (Chicago?) to San Jose. We would both arrive at different times. We were expected to manage luggage and so on individually, at our age, through this long journey.

Finally, when we refused this arrangement, BA staff were kind to find seats for us both on a flight the next day, leaving at the same time, but then going from London through Chicago to SJ, this adding another 6 hours to the already long journey.

At the end of all this, we finally made it to San Jose.

I was wondering whether airlines like BA think about the mental tension of old people when they make

- such last-minute changes
- offer solutions that are not practical
- remain ignorant of the inconvenience of going back to a locked home and of
- making one more trip from the Mumbai suburb of Chembur to the airport, the next day, and the expenses involved.

There was not even a hint of some compensation for the inconvenience and the expenses. Is this normal? Or does one have to ask for it, in a formal way?

I had earlier decided to ignore this incident, but then I was made to wait a full hour at the check in at the BA counter in San Jose.

On September 10, 2018, when my wife and I were returning, just because they could not get the passport details through (whatever that means) because the machine was not working efficiently, and even the wheelchair attendant would not wait for me to finish, I had enough.

I decided I must put all this down on paper and inform those who are distant from the scene of action in the BA office, so they can take some action, now, and to prevent such situations in the future.

So I tried to send an e-mail message—bounced!

I spent time to call on their advertised telephone number. No one picking up the phone.

I gave up!

(I was writing to Swati- so, as a travel agent, she could follow up. Perhaps, they may be more receptive to a travel agent, since a lot of future business is involved)

Sinha's Experience with SAS: Good Customer Value Creation

Sonny Sinha had just finished his PhD in solid state nuclear physics at Cambridge. He had decided to marry a girl from Scandinavia, who he had met on campus, and he was traveling on a Saturday for his wedding on Sunday. At the airport in London he realizes he does not have formal shoes for the wedding (absentminded professor–scientist). He looks around—no shoe shop. He goes to the SAS counter for help. They agree. There is no shoe shop at Heathrow. Too bad, he thought, he will have to make do with sports shoes. He would not be able to buy on a Sunday before the time for the wedding!

Imagine his surprise when he landed in Copenhagen—his name was announced. He went to the SAS counter. Any problem? No. There was a parcel with black leather shoes for him and a bouquet of flowers for his bride—from SAS.

Since that time, Sinha has become a world-class figure in the nuclear field, addressing five to six conferences every year in different parts of the world. He always travels SAS—unless SAS has no service to that destination. SAS has created a customer for life, not with a pair of shoes and a bouquet of flowers, but with thoughtfulness, concern, empathy!

Gautam's experience with Airlines

People are getting edgy and are shifting around. Why is the plane not leaving the gate. It is already half an hour since the plane was to depart. Some ask the steward, who says he will find out. Never comes back. No announcements, as the delay creeps to 1 hour. The captain comes on but the voice is crackling and he is barely heard. I ask my young neighbor, and he says one instrument was not working and is being replaced. We should be on our way in 5 minutes. Those 5 minutes stretch.

Don't airlines realize they have us captive in the plane. We cannot jump off. Don't they realize we can get anxious and worried, especially if we have planned a meeting based on timely arrival. Don't they realize we want to hear what they are saying.

Why are all airlines like this? Why are they casual about this? Are they casual about other things like safety? I wonder.

All of our readers have been through this. Isn't this an easily solvable problem by all airlines with an "I care attitude"? Do they really care?

This is best answered when things go wrong. Your flight is canceled, overly delayed, lands at the wrong airport. How are you treated then?

A welcome change- Indian Airlines and Air India

Good Customer Value Creation

During the flooding of Mumbai airport in 2005 it was closed for a few days and I (Gautam) was one of the persons stuck at the airport. All the private airline personnel went home leaving their passengers stranded. Only Indian Airlines had a fully (maybe more than fully) staffed terminal, and they had gotten in water and refreshments and arranged buses for people to go to Hotel Orchid for dinner, an example of great caring, normally not displayed. The staff was outstanding in their support and help. I wrote about this and the article appeared in 23 newspapers. I wrote to the CEO of Indian Airlines, and got no response.

Indian Airlines gave another outstanding example of Creating Value. There used to be a hopping flight, Delhi–Baroda–Ahmedabad–Delhi. The flight was late coming in from Delhi. We boarded the plane at Baroda, and were given permission to fly even though we were past the curfew time (no flying after 7 p.m.).

The flight landed in Ahmedabad, and we were hoping to get to Delhi, albeit late. Unluckily, the crew had been flying for over 8 hours and had to get off the plane. There was no other crew available in Ahmedabad.

It was past midnight. The passengers including me were asked to get off the plane, and in the terminal building there was only one young man from Air India (then known as Indian Airlines). He managed, in spite of shouting passengers, to get buses and hotel rooms for all of us. We were in different hotels, and were told a special flight would come the next day to pick us up. At 10 a.m. the flight arrived and we got home.

Here is yet another example of Air India. I was to take a flight from Delhi to Jakarta via Chennai and Singapore, where I would change planes.

As we left Delhi, the weather got worse and rains lashed at us. We were forced to land in Hyderabad, which is short of Chennai by 300 miles. We were asked whether we wanted to stay at the airport, on the plane (just in case the weather eased), or at a hotel. I opted to stay on the plane.

Next morning we headed back to Delhi, where I was put on the next flight (this one was Singapore Air) to Singapore. The flight was late. I had been booked on an Air India flight from Singapore to Jakarta. When I got off the plane I asked the ground crew (all Singapore Airlines people) if they could help me catch the flight to Jakarta. They were most unhelpful and said impossible.

I was walking down the corridor when I saw the flight status monitor, which said the Air India flight would leave in 20 minutes. So I ran to the gate. I was a business class passenger. The fellow at the desk (a Singapore Air rep) was most rude and sort of said how dare you come so late. Anyway, I got on the Air India flight and complained to the purser about the treatment at the gate. The purser told me they are quite rude and many of our passengers have complained. So much for Value Starvation from Singapore Airlines.

The last SA incident is an example of Customer Value Starvation, the rest of Value Starvation/Destruction.

Jet Airways

Jet changed the flight timing to Jodhpur for January 2, 2019, but announcing this in November 2018 to 2 and one half hours later. This would cause us to be late for a meeting. I had read somewhere that a ruling by Directorate General of Civil Aviation (DGCA), travelers could ask for the earlier flight with no cancelation charges and no extra charges for the earlier flight, if available (even if the fare is higher).

I tried to cancel the flight, or change it. Jet wanted a huge cancelation charge. Fortunately, I knew a senior VP at Jet, and wrote to him, and my problem was solved right away.

Why do people make it difficult for customers to get their rights? Can this be rectified by training?

Lessons from the Stories Above

The problem is that frontline staff become mouth pieces of the company and often do not have recourse to higher-ups. (Try asking a frontline staff to connect you to a decision maker. He cannot and will not, as he is also made the gatekeeper.) Try getting real help. You cannot. This is also a case of Value Starvation.

Airports

Most of us know the kind of services provided at airports, especially in India. The entry to the airport is a problem. Queues are long because the two guards take time to read names on the ticket and then relate them to the identity card. Yes, they now want an original ID, so in the pell-mell at the airport if you lose it (as happened to me), *bad luck*.

There are times when the immigration counters have long queues at each counter, so that the time it takes to go through can be a good portion of the flight time (a 1-hour wait for a 3-hour flight). Yet, out of the eight counters, 3 are unmanned. No personnel on duty and therefore no solution available at short notice. Customer Value Starvation. This is unlike Dubai or Singapore, where personnel are allocated to empty counters soon after the authorities realize that the crowd is unusually large. Customer Value Creation.

Example of Good Customer Care

Walter received this letter from Expedia. Airlines are giving flexible fares in selected dates in March 2020.

Dear Walter,

We know the recent news and uncertainty surrounding the coronavirus (COVID-19) may have you taking a deeper look into your current travel plans and future options. Whether you already have a trip booked or are looking ahead for upcoming travel, we wanted to let you know that we're working daily to assess any new impacts and updates to travel policies to keep you informed.

Travel disruptions can be difficult, and we understand that your time and personal well-being are critically important. If you already booked travel with us, please know we're working hard to resolve individual issues based on the policies set forth by our partners. We realize there have been areas where we have been unable to directly assist you and we're working to fix that in the near future. If you have general questions about your options, we encourage you to visit our online **Customer Service Portal** to help manage your upcoming trip.

If you are planning ahead for future travel, rest assured we are working closely with our partners to make sure you have as much flexibility as possible. For a limited time, several airlines including American Airlines, Alaska Airlines, Delta Air Lines, JetBlue and United Airlines are waiving change fees on select flights booked in March. In addition, most of our hotels already offer free cancellation options for maximum flexibility if your plans change.

We are working around the clock to ensure we respond to updates as they occur. We hope that by sharing information with you as the situation evolves, we can help you navigate through this time and provide peace of mind for your next trip.

Sincerely,
Expedia Travel Team
To learn more about flexible booking and the travel protection we offer, visit our **COVID-19 travel advice page.**

Gautam's comments: I had been booked on a British Airways flight for April 6, 2020, through Expedia; the flight was canceled due to the Covid-19 virus. First, Expedia told me to talk to BA. Now neither will refund my money but are saying the money can be used for a subsequent flight. What if I do not want to fly? What happens? Who can help me and remove my Customer Value Starvation?

As a footnote I got the refund 5 months later.

Observations of Customer Value Starvation—At Home

Construction Quality

In many parts of the world, Customer Value Starvation starts with our homes and our offices. Between the two, this is where we spend most of our time. The November 12, 2018 issue of the *Times of India* reported that at the prestigious Indian Institute of Technology in Mumbai, chunks of slab fell in a student's hostel room. The student was not on the bed at the time of the incident, thus escaping any major injury. Students claimed that the chunks were huge and sturdy, with sharp edges. There was a similar incident 2 weeks earlier in another room in the same hostel. The hostel was built only 10 years ago; yet, it seems to be going to pieces. The complaint is that the contractors do not get time to do the maintenance because the hostels are always occupied, even during the holidays, since there are internship programs going on. But should a hostel built only 10 years ago need such major renovations? This is a question one has to ask.

These companies and institutes must learn safety is a form of customer value and trust. If you provide unsafe accommodations, you will destroy value.

How were such structures designed by contractors? How were they approved and permitted by government authorities? Who will be responsible to take the rap, in case of injuries or deaths?

And this is true for all buildings, not just the hostel of the institute. Strict liability laws with criminal action may reduce this, provided corrupt people do not prevent this.

And Gautam adds,

Many years ago, I was staying at a Tata company guesthouse. There were a group of DuPont (from Wimington, De, USA) people doing a safety audit. I asked them at breakfast if they thought the guesthouse was safe. They said this was outside their scope. Things like first-aid kits, anti-skid bathrooms were missing and were a case in point. Should someone get a cut (or the cook gets a big gash), you can't dress it.

Fire Safety

In a guesthouse for seniormost executives belonging to a major Indian company, where I stayed one night, I noticed there were iron grills on the windows and doors, preventing ingress and escape from the guesthouse. In the morning I wanted to go for a walk. The only entrance/exit was barred (with bars), and I had to wait for the caretaker to return.

I thought to myself if there is a fire, we are all going to be fried, as there is no openable exit. The sad part is the CXOs did not notice/did not care. I told the company I would never stay in this guesthouse again because of safety. I do not know if they instituted any change.

Should we not expect owners of offices and property developers to provide us with fire contingencies, or ensure approach roads where fire engines can drive in, in any contingency?

There are many examples of people dying of fire, such as the three residents who died when there was a minor fire in their eight-floor building in suburban Mumbai. By the time the fire engines could come, and the fire controlled, the three were already dead.

You look at the new high-rise buildings in Mumbai, some as high as 48 floors. Should there be a fire, is the fire brigade of Mumbai equipped to fight fires at that height? What would happen in a 48-floor building, if there is a similar calamity, is anyone's guess. A clear case of Customer Value Starvation.

Water Supply

Have we not had property developers cheat us on built-up area; by allowing permission to occupy without NOC (No Objection Certificate) from the Municipal Corporation; by not making sure there is regular water supply or hygienic water?

Most of the buildings in many parts of India have no direct water supply. They rely on water tankers, making it inconvenient and expensive for residents—a clear case of Customer Value Starvation.

How do authorities give approvals for construction of buildings, and especially high-rise ones, in areas where there is no water supply and will not be available in the foreseeable future?

The ignorant buyers of property also do not check this aspect and are in for an unpleasant surprise when they have to buy water from water tankers at a high cost, an expense they had not budgeted for.

There is the problem of no supply, and there is the problem of polluted water supply. It is contaminated water for 42 percent of the urban and 60 percent of the rural population. Sure the rural population has wells, but many of them are contaminated by the pesticides used on farms to improve crop yields and therefore get into another kind of problem, that of polluted drinking water!

Home Delivery

Have you ever wondered why Indian delivery teams, whether from Amazon, Croma, courier services, or even taxi services such as Ola and Meru, never know how to reach your location to deliver or pick up? This goes for service people from printers, air conditioners, water systems, and so on.

They all call to ask your address and have no idea where it is. (Why can't the company provide that information?)

They want directions, but are not trained to take them. They call back after a few minutes and ask again. And again!

A waste of time causing Customer Value Starvation.

This is lost time and lost productivity for the company and costs them money. It is wasted time for the customer.

Don't companies understand this?

As an afternote, it appears delivery people are calling us less for directions.

Observations of Customer Value Starvation— Outside the Home

The Pavement/Road

When one walks out of the building onto the pavement, one still walks alongside the risks. On November 16, 2018, the *Times of India* reported that a senior citizen, who had gone out to buy flowers to offer at a temple, had fallen down on an uneven road in the Tilak Nagar suburb of Mumbai. It was the same spot that her husband had complained about earlier, to the civic authorities. But nothing was done. They later found that something had been done—the pavement instead of the road had been repaired!

And this is true for many, many roads in Mumbai and many other large cities in the country. It is where civic authorities indulge in Customer Value Starvation on a massive scale.

Are pavements made for pedestrian use and their safety? One would have thought so, but the number of pavements where the civic authorities allow stalls and force pedestrians to walk on the road itself exposes them to great danger. Yet, the stalls are there for all to see. There may be complaints filed, but they are studiously ignored. When business increases, the mobile stalls set up brick and mortar structures and become permanent—on the pavement. Pedestrian, please make way. We have arrived.

How does this happen? Connivance and cooperation between the lawmakers and the law breakers, with money changing hands, to the detriment of the common citizen, who looks on helplessly at these exercises in Customer Value Starvation!

The number of accidents on the pavements in our cities is testimony of the poor quality of the construction. The paver blocks are not placed neatly. Some even come out and leave a hole (or holes). Older people venturing out, even at their slow pace, face a danger every day.

A recent report in the press stated that potholes on roads kill more people per year than the ultras (terrorists) do! And the Supreme Court of India says the authorities must compensate every victim.

It is said that every fatal road accident leaves at least three to four persons injured and many of them become bedridden for the rest of their lives.

India Today has said there are over 9,300 deaths, 25,000 injured in 3 years due to potholes.

Road Safety Design Should Take into Account Driver Error

The World Bank and National Highways Authority of India have found that many national highways in India are unsafe for vehicles. Some highways are up to 50 percent unsafe for vehicles. National Highways are important to India, as they carry 40 percent plus of the traffic. They also account for 35 percent of fatalities. This is Customer Value Starvation, when the roads slow you down or damage your car, but is value destruction if someone dies.

Authorities must change their thought process on safety to avoid deaths. Part of the problem is our driver licensing program, which is weak. Driver training is important. In the United States, professional drivers are proud of their profession. In India, professional drivers are the worst culprits with a *do not care* attitude. Such Value Starvation by the driver causing accidents has to be dealt with as a serious issue.

Pollution

Having stepped out of the home and onto the street and having managed to keep our balance on uneven roads and pavements, the next challenge is the air we breathe. This is one more form of Value Starvation.

The pollution levels have gone so high, that we are forced to take in increasing doses of pollutants in the air we breathe, and no amount of yogic breathing exercises are going to be able to fight this major battle for all humanity.

Every day, one has to check what the pollution index is in the major cities of India. Generally, the first prize goes to Delhi, the highest level of pollution. In fact, so high, that some embassies have recalled staff back to headquarters because of the health issue. In the meantime, various theories are put forward about why the pollution level is so high. The large number of transport vehicles? The use of diesel engines? The burning of post-harvest stubble in distant Haryana, by farmers? The Covid-19 experience has shown us that air pollution can be reduced substantially with no traffic.

The situation is not much better in some other countries like China. With affluence, the roads of Beijing are teeming with cars, rather than with bicycles, as in the recent past. But there are others like Singapore, who have made it so difficult to own a car, and made public transport so convenient and comfortable, that Singapore can have clean air. Even then, the pollution breezing down in its direction from Indonesia may negate its efforts to some extent. There is also the example of the Scandinavian countries, which have taken measures that are prophylactic, rather than therapeutic, to become *iconic* examples of how to manage pollution.

In the meantime, most of the poor in developing countries will die before their time, and never know why. The rich in these countries will opt for yogic breathing exercise if they are so inclined. Others will buy air purifiers and install in their homes and offices and even in their cars. Manufacturers will have a field day, diversifying from marketing water purifiers to also market air purifiers, and improving the balance sheet.

And top management (civic authorities/government) will pretend that the problem does not exist!

During the Covid pandemic, we found that air pollution had fallen because of lower number of cars on the road and lower manufacturing. So had water pollution (the Yamuna River in Delhi was at its cleanest, and the beaches in Goa were pristine).

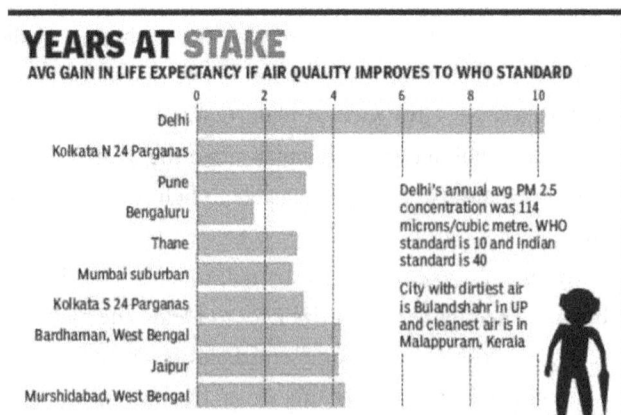

YEARS AT STAKE
AVG GAIN IN LIFE EXPECTANCY IF AIR QUALITY IMPROVES TO WHO STANDARD

Delhi's annual avg PM 2.5 concentration was 114 microns/cubic metre. WHO standard is 10 and Indian standard is 40

City with dirtiest air is Bulandshahr in UP and cleanest air is in Malappuram, Kerala

https://timesofindia.indiatimes.com/city/delhi/foul-air-reducing-delhiites-life-by-10-years-study/articleshow/66700240.cms

Is it too much to expect clean air? Yet, foul air seems to engulf the country from North to South.

Foul air is reducing life expectancy in Delhi by as much as 10 years.

Is this not a matter of grave concern?

And some parts of Mumbai are even more polluted than Delhi.

What We Eat

A global nutrition report says that what we are eating is killing us. Diets are one of the top risk factors of mortality in the world, more than even air pollution.

"What We're Eating Is Killing Us": Global Nutrition Report

Poor diet and unhygienic food cause one in five deaths, according to the Global Nutrition Report. What we eat is killing us and is a major cause of death and illnesses. Malnutrition is a form of value, and literal, starvation. Such malnutrition probably costs $4 trillion a year, according to some reports. There is a cost associated with Value Starvation.

We can overcome some of this by installing clean and safe drinking fountains and restricting unhealthy food advertising. We should promote healthy snacks and guidance for healthy snacks in schools.

Another form of Customer Value Starvation is food waste, which must be reduced. This includes cooked food and fresh fruits and vegetables that are wasted or rot.

Because of this, the Global Food Safety rules are being revised and hopefully will be adopted by 185 nations. Will the situation improve? One hopes so.

Other examples are given in http://cercindia.org/category/latest-test-report/

Out of 12 lipsticks tested, 4 were found to have shockingly high levels of arsenic, and out of 12 brands of *kajal* tested, 2 were found to have very high levels of lead (refer to CERC India). Would you want these on your lips and eyes?

Turmeric is so widely used in cooking in India, and 80 percent of packed and loose turmeric sold in the market was found to be adulterated (refer to CERC reports).

At present nearly 80 percent of the milk in the state of Maharashtra is substandard. This is in spite of having a leading, reputed milk product like Amul.

Eating chicken could make you antibiotic resistant. Antibiotics are pumped to make chicken plumper.

Study Found "Multiantibiotic"-Resistant Bacteria in Chicken Samples from Mumbai

There is an urgent need to limit antibiotic use and stop antibiotic misuse for poultry, says study co-author. Consuming antibiotic- treated chicken can cause humans who consume such chicken to lose immunity. Humans who need antibiotics do not get any relief because the antibiotics do not work. So when we eat such chicken there is Customer Value Starvation on our health.

The Centre for Science and Environment (CSE), a Delhi-based non-profit, had highlighted the misuse and overuse of antibiotics in poultry farming in India as growth promoters and has been advocating the need to eliminate nontherapeutic antibiotic use in animals.

In 2014, the Union agriculture ministry issued an advisory for not using antibiotics in feed or feed supplements for animals but it is voluntary and hence unenforceable. The Bureau of Indian Standards (BIS) also recommends not using antibiotics with systemic action as growth promoters in feed. However, this is again not mandatory.

Packaged Foods Contaminated

About 60 to 80 percent of food in plastic bags is contaminated in some way or the other. Poor raw materials, unapproved additives and dyes, poor sterilization or pasteurization, and worse still, poor packaging materials that do not comply with standards are a cause of Value Starvation. An example is Bisphenol A found in baby bottles used to feed babies.

New Food Packaging Regulations were to have been complied with by all food businesses by July 1, 2019.

This will protect the food contents from microbiological, chemical, physical, and atmospheric contamination and will preserve the food.

It is the same with contamination of drinking water packed in plastic containers of a lower quality and exposed for long periods to sunlight and heat. Maybe we can reduce the Value Starvation?

Local Transport

And when one has finished shopping and managed to get an autorickshaw, one may find that rigged meters have made a comeback. One has now to hope for the RTO (Regional Transport Office) to be more active, for consumers to be more vocal, and for the RTO to replace e-meters with GPS meters that will automatically calculate fare based on real time, and GPS enabled distance and waiting time.

Five autorickshaw drivers are booked on an average every week for rigged electronic meters in the eastern and western suburbs, according to latest statistics released by the Maharashtra state transport department. "When electronic meters were introduced a few years back, we presumed that tampering was not possible." Unscrupulous drivers use an adaptor that inflates the distance traveled reading by 30 to 40 percent. Such Customer Value Starvation can be avoided by using the new GPS meters.

Financial Services—Banks and Insurance

Many customers have endless problems with banks. Part of the reason is that bank employees (relationship managers) have targets to be achieved. To achieve these targets they push products that may be unsuitable to the consumer. Thus, one gets stuck with a problem from which it is not easy to come out in the short term.

TataAIG and the Catch 22 for travel insurance: These are two examples of Customer Value Starvation.

The first has to do with overseas travel insurance. If you are an American resident in India, you cannot fill in the complete U.S. passport number on the form. So your number is incomplete and therefore wrong. Right below this it says that any false information will make this policy null and void. I have been doing this for 4 years now, and have talked to a senior VP, who arranges to send me an endorsement letter with the full passport number. The problem was not fixed permanently. Why not stop starving other customers also?

If you have an overseas medical policy, you are supposed to pay medical bills and then ask for reimbursement, unless you are admitted into a hospital. I was not admitted into a hospital where I went to. I gave my insurance policy number to the hospital. All I got from the hospital was that payment was due, and I was delinquent. When I asked for bills, they said they had sent bills to the insurance company and could not send me bills till the claim was denied. The insurance company was doing nothing. When I asked them what I should do they said I should pay (which I could not do in the absence of bills) and then I would be reimbursed. Finally, I went to a friend in the company who arranged for cashless payment.

Health Insurance

Value Starvation from a huge Indian company: Keep the customer in the dark

For the last 7 days I have been trying to pay my health insurance policy to HDFC ERGO.

As a background, the company apparently changed the attributes for the policy after they had sent me a renewal notice with their old rates. I have three policies: one for my wife, one for my son, and one for myself.

They agreed to hold my rates. I tried to pay online. I was told I could not do so and to call a number.

I went to their e-mail that had the renewal notice; 'the click this' to pay now option gave me an error message when I tried to pay.

Then I called the call center, and they said I would hear from the renewal team.

The renewal team sent me three text messages, each with a reference number, a link, and an amount. With the reference number I have no idea which policy they are referring to, as my wife and I have the same premium amount. Unfortunately, the premium was for the new amount. The amount for my wife and myself had gone up by 70 percent (and I still do not know what I am getting in return in terms of enhancements).

My son's policy had gone up a whopping 17 times, and again, with no explanation.

To cut a long story short, after making a lot of noise I got three text messages with reference numbers. Unfortunately, links were for two policies, and the third had no link. I paid two policies on the reference number and still do not know whose they are as the receipt only gives a reference number.

Why does this happen?

The attitude is not to solve a problem permanently. Only the top people can do this. They pass the problem on to the next layer of people, who are doing their job routinely with no thought applied. Why is the reference number not linked to the policy number so that the customer knows what he is paying for? Why is there no link in one SMS? Is this a quality control problem or plain sloppiness? How can all this be avoided? Why does the new amount keep appearing? Why is there no communication between departments to avoid this? Who is going to make the changes for the future?

Apart from this, why is the company highhanded? Why not tell us: Dear customer, we are making a change in our policy offering; these are the changes and this is why it will cost more. They could also say the old policy offerings are no longer valid. Give me a choice to stay on or go elsewhere.

I do realize part of this problem is arising because software has not kept up with people who were allowed to stay with the old policy.

And after that do make sure I do not have problems paying.

After all this I get a customer satisfaction (CSAT) or Customer satisfaction questionnaire. How should I rate them?

Do companies realize how much of their time and the customer's time is wasted and how much it costs them to correct these problems?

I hope you will not have such issues.

Insurance Agents

Perhaps many insurance agents have been mainly responsible in giving insurance—whether life or health insurance—a bad name. My own experience with insurance agents, except for one, has not been very good. I remember them to be persistent with visits and phone calls until you give them the check. After that, one is removed from the *call list,* except when it is time for the next premium to be paid. And the agent is never to be seen again!

Health insurance companies are known for making sure that there is sufficient deduction from the claim. For me, the last situation was when my claim for reimbursement of operation expenses was reduced to make items like surgical gloves, bandages, and other items used in surgery as *not allowable*. Can one do a surgery without gloves, cotton, and bandages? Questioning the insurance company only gives them an excuse to delay the payment. You know it is unfair but instead of wasting time, you just take the check for what is approved and move on. Most times, medical insurance means an exercise in Customer Value Starvation.

HDFC Bank: Here are problems I have had. They scramble the keyboard and you have to search for a letter. After each letter, the system gets rescrambled so you have to look again. By the time you end they say you are timed out!

And then if you did not use the bank website in 3 months, your password is blocked, and you have to go through a rigmarole to get a new password.

Happy to say things have improved now.

Here are two more peeves. Try reaching the relationship manager....

I bank at the GK2 branch. When you look for the branch in the drop-down menu, it is not there. Finally, I learned it was under Masjid Moth. You are supposed to know your geography to bank with HDFC.

I used to know many VPs at the bank, and they all heard me patiently...but nothing happens or changes.

Is Your Bank Mis-selling?

In an era in which one reads about multiple bank frauds that have hit the cooperative sector hard and even some of the larger banks, a result of lack of control in managing the banks and especially their lending policies (Customer Value Starvation), it is good to see India's largest bank (the State Bank of India [SBI]) has decided to refund the borrower if the construction project is delayed.

But this is the only silver lining to a scenario of dark clouds. The lack of a uniform regulatory and supervisory structure and dishonest management have contributed to a series of bank scams. One of the biggest in recent times has been that of the Punjab and Maharashtra Co-operative (PMC) bank. Depositors have lost their life's savings. Some have even committed suicide in desperation. Yet, the authorities remain unmoved, and seem clueless about what to do. And, as if PMC was not enough, YES Bank soon followed for the same reason. Bad loans will continue to stress many banks and consequently give sleepless nights to the banks' customers.

The consolation is that India is not alone. Australia's financial giants, Commonwealth, Westpac, and ANZ, are among the world's most profitable financial institutions. Australia sailed through the world's 2008 financial crisis unscathed, unlike banks in the United States and Europe. Yet, now, Australia's scandal plagued banks are accused of putting profit before people and failing to meet "basic standards of honesty."

The 1,000-page Royal Commission Report painted a picture of a sector defined by greed, forgiving of misconduct, and frequently flirting with illegality. Asking why this happened, the report concludes that, too often, the answer seems to be greed. It goes to detail examples of cash-stuffed envelopes being taken to pass dubious loans and fees being charged to customers who died up to a decade earlier!

The commission also accused government regulators of being asleep at the wheel. Much of this information was published by the print edition of the *South China Morning Post*, "Greedy banks pilloried in scathing inquiry report."

Reserve Bank of India (RBI)

The RBI is the repository of all banks and is supposed to set an example for them. In fact, I have spoken and given courses to various banks at the RBI College in Pune on creating Customer Value.

This happened a few days ago. I decided to buy Government of India taxable bonds. I could not apply online (notice RBI talks about digitization of service). You have to fill in a form.

If you are applying for a joint holdership, you are both asked to sign on the second page. On subsequent pages, it says signature of first holder but they insist on both holders when you submit the form (why can't they say so?). You are asked to fill in check details such as name of bank, account number, and IFSC code. This should be sufficient. But no, they want the MICR code. And all this a number of times. And to receive NEFT (wireless) payment, you have to fill in an application to the receiving bank to receive this money. Never heard of such poppycock in today's day and age.

My bank allows me to sign checks up to a limit of Rs. 10 lakh. So to put in Rs 50 lakh I have to fill in five forms. Why can't I send five checks with one application form?

And I have to sign the canceled check and my identity card photocopies. One copy will not suffice. I need five copies.

And don't RBI officials notice this, or are they above all of this? Wilful Value Starvation or uncaring Value Starvation or unwitting Value Starvation?

Railways

Does it need several decades and thousands of *accident deaths* where passengers fall between the train and the tracks before bringing in a simple correction of increasing the platform height by 900 mm, so someone will not be able to fall through? Yet, this is what has happened.

Having automatic closing doors on trains may be a longer term solution and a more expensive one. But raising platforms, especially at crowded stations, is something that can easily be done.

Pic used for representation only

DEATHS ON SUBURBAN RLY NETWORK

HC ON FATAL FALLS

In our view the principal reason why these accidents take place, more particularly the reason why commuters fall down from the train, is the overcrowding of trains at peak hours. We expect the railway authorities to set up a research team to find a suitable solution ...

RLYS FOR 15-CAR RAKES

➤ WR has said platform extension for 15 coaches between Andheri and Virar will happen by Aug 2020
➤ CR says 15-car rakes use all stations between CSMT and Kalyan except Vikhroli (but not on slow tracks)

DEATHS FROM FALLING OFF TRAIN

Year	Deaths	Total Deaths
2015	806	(3,304 Total Deaths)
2016	657	(3,202)
2017	654	(3,014)
2018	711	(2,981)

An example of Value Starvation is poor food quality on the railways, whether it is stale bread or moldy food (multiple complaints on various train routes). My friend Larry Malarkar would say if all of this is one off, then it is a service lapse and service recovery is the solution. I agree, except if it happens without being noticed and is allowed to continue, it becomes Customer Value Starvation. And the problem is most customers and even staff do not notice, and if brought to their notice, they shrug and continue to ignore it. Larry suggests that training can change this. This is true if the problem is noticed and then a plan of action can ensue. That is why I say awareness is very important.

Customer Value Starvation is common with the service of the railways. If not the crowds in the unreserved compartments, then it is the moldy bread served by the catering, or the spoiled *pulav* (fried rice) served on the high-class Tejas train, which operates between Goa and Mumbai and about which there have been complaints even in the press.

If you are tech savvy, you can now book tickets on the Internet, as a lot of progress has been made over the years, to make things easier, including the facility to buy tickets for long-distance travel at suburban railway stations or the post office. This is Customer Value Creation. However, for the masses, booking a ticket on the railways for a long-distance journey, at short notice, is still difficult, namely, long queues and the tempting presence of touts, who can get a ticket for you immediately. Customer Value Starvation.

Indian Railways, both suburban and long distance, continue to be weighed under Customer Value Starvation, though there are initiatives now taken, like the new Tejas train, Mumbai to Ahmedabad, where passengers will receive Rs. 100 each if the train is delayed.

Holiday Resorts

Customer Value Starvation—and Mahindra Holidays (MH)

In July 2018, my wife and I were going abroad and we were pushed into buying forex currency of over $1,000 each from HDFC, which was our banker. The attraction was that for every forex card, when you buy currency of over $1,000, you would be eligible for a bonus of 2 nights and 3 days at a Mahindra resort. It seemed a good offer. We both fell for it. Both of us were enthused. We were also members of Club Mahindra and so it was familiar territory. There was no time limit mentioned in the original announcement.

We were away on and off for many months, and in April 2019, we submitted the vouchers for redemption. No response from MH. We spoke to the relationship manager from HDFC bank. He said he will try and sort out the problem. Then no news. I rang up MH. Every time there was a different person on the phone; every time repeating the same story: The matter has been transferred to the head office in Chennai. Mumbai office cannot handle this and take a decision. Many telephone calls between April and September 2019—yet, nothing done. It was just a matter of four nights, as an offer, not an earth-shaking decision to be taken.

But like many companies, MH had decided to resort to Customer Value Starvation. On the one hand, they were busy Creating Value by expanding the range of resorts. On the other hand, they were unconsciously driving away existing customers. Customer Value Creation was being counterbalanced by Customer Value Starvation.

The result: When MH advertises cruise gifts for enrolling new members, one wonders whether this is another hoax, to cheat the unsuspecting customer.

The trust is broken. Customer Value Starvation has captured another victim!

Shep Hyken's principle: "Every negative situation is an opportunity to learn"—whether in restaurants, airlines, software services, or corporate culture management.

Customer Value Starvation and Companies

Are Older and Established Organizations Better at Avoiding Customer Value Starvation?

In theory, large and long-established organizations should have more experience. They know what to do, and what not to do. They would have learned by being burnt by the fire of customer irritation, and sometimes, customer migration.

Yet, most times, this does not happen. The following happens:

The larger a company becomes, the further its top management gets from the ultimate customer. The number of layers of personnel increases, until the top management gets isolated and insulated from the ultimate customer.

And many of the reports in the general press show how true this is.

We have always sworn by German technology and their preoccupation with perfection. And among the German hi-tech companies, Volkswagen (VW) was among the stars. Yet, what finally happened? VW had to recall thousands of cars in the United States, because they did not meet safety standards, even though the Standards Department had released these cars for sale! What a letdown! A complete betrayal of confidence. (And this has happened again, with Toyota—which is also a shame.)

Sometimes, you can get outstanding service, but this is often not orchestrated from the top.

Unfortunately, companies want to be able to contact customers but not have customers contact them conveniently. Companies seem to say keep away; you cannot contact me. They set up the one-way contact system.

Also unfortunate that the convenience of the company takes precedence over the convenience of the customer.

Lastly, companies are taking over the customer's rights by insisting on their submitting the customers location, their pictures, and so on when customers sign into their website or app. A case of aggravated privacy loss, and Value Starvation (because you are forced to give information and spend time). Sometimes Google or one of the biggies will take over your system and keep reminding you to use them. It is irritating and causes Customer Value Starvation.

The Critical Role of Follow-up to Prevent Customer Value Starvation

Walter's comments:

When I look at the buildings in Hong Kong or the roads in Dubai, the uniform architecture of buildings in different parts of London or on the islands of Greece, and then return to India and compare the scenario, I wonder why the great disparity. Except for a few patches in this vast country, India is a potpourri! Finally, after much thought, I have come to the following conclusion:

The key to success in many of these of these areas is the ability to effectively follow up.

*Why do buildings show dangerous cracks after just 10 years of being built in India?

Because there has not been sufficient supervision of the concrete mixing process or the curing during construction. Instructions have been given but there is no proper supervision and follow-up to see that these processes were done as instructed.

*Why do we realize that there is not sufficient room for fire engines to come to the 48th floor of a building in South Mumbai, only in case of a fire?

Because there was no follow-up to check on this aspect by the supervising engineers of the contractors or the supervising engineers of the municipality, after the construction was complete. They did not check whether all rules had been followed, before the NOC (No Objection Certificate of the municipality) was given, and the flat owners moved in.

*Why are there potholes on roads that have recently been repaired?

Because the road engineers of the municipality gave instructions and then never visited the site to check during or after the laying of the road.

Was the mixture right? Was the laying right? Was the area cordoned off so that there was sufficient time for the tar/cement to dry and solidify? It cannot be. Because most times even on cement roads, there are footprints of people who have walked on the soft cement. Obviously, the area was not cordoned off, to keep pedestrians away while the cement was setting!

*Why are the floor tiles laid with wider spaces between tiles (a repository for dirt), while in Hong Kong or Dubai, the interstitial spaces are hardly noticed? *Can it be because of a lack of supervision and not insisting on performance close to perfection?*

After all, it is often Indian laborers who do this job in Dubai, as they do in India. So what is different? Is it the supervision, the follow-up?

It was such a relief to see the Municipal Council in Mumbai organize the removal of slums from the pavements of both sides on a main artery road like P. D'Mello Road in South Mumbai.

This was miles of pavements with thousands of people who considered these as semipermanent residences, even acquiring color TV sets and arrangements for supply of containers of water. Now, the pavements are clean and dry, and it has been a pleasure to drive down the road. However, a few hutments have now sprung up here and there. There is no follow-up to the clearance campaign. The danger is that P. D'Mello Road may return to the status quo ante.

Why do successors to MAFCO stalls make these stalls permanent?

There was a time when the government milk dairy—MAFCO—was allowed to put up stalls on pavements, to create a wide distribution network to distribute milk to citizens, even in down-market areas. After many years, the MAFCO scheme has been discontinued. But the wooden temporary stalls have been taken over by private entrepreneurs, who are now selling snacks and juices and have transformed them from wooden stalls to brick and mortar. Now these stalls will be permanently on the pavements, which were primarily for the use of pedestrians, specially the old and the disabled.

Why does this happen? No follow-up, causing Customer Value Starvation for the common man, who will be expected to keep paying taxes for services he is not provided, but should have expected.

What are the campaigns being held at regular intervals to check hygiene standards in hotels and restaurants?

Yes, these are held at regular intervals. And the inspectors have a field day tasting excellent food at excellent restaurants. The inspectors neither have the time nor the inclination to check on the quality of food at the thousands of roadside stalls serving snacks like *vada pao* or juices like sugarcane juice in the most unhygienic surroundings. There is no follow-up in the areas where it is needed most, again causing Customer Value Starvation.

Must we have tall Manhattan-style buildings in a crumbling 100-year-old neighborhood?

You have to look at parts of Mumbai, and perhaps, most other cities and towns in India. You see tall elegant buildings, sometimes 40-floors high, surrounded by crumbling, unpainted 2- and 3-storey houses that are between 50 and 80 years old. This shows complete *dissonance and architectural conflict* in the area. And all because there is a lack of follow-up by town planners, who will not learn from the great care and taste that town planners show in similar situations in countries like Singapore.

For news channels, it is headline today—to be forgotten a week later.

Every day, it is a challenge to have a new and earth-shaking headline. There is news of a politician or a well-known bureaucrat caught for corruption, and cases being filed. The person is sent to jail. Most times he finds a way to spend most of the time in hospital, because now, as an accused, he does not keep good health—until the whole story is forgotten and the politician quietly slides into a comfortable retirement, or is back in circulation and even becomes a minister again! What happened? No one knows because there has been no follow-up by the media, and for that matter, many consumers don't notice or don't care.

Lack of a fast, effective justice system makes citizens bitter.

Customer Value Starvation is possibly highest in our justice system. It is said that 68 percent of our jails are filled by under-trial prisoners. They could be there for years. Why? Because the justice system is so slow. It is unfair to those who are detained (especially, if after 7 years, the prisoner is found to be innocent). But who cares? There is no quick follow-up system nor any timelines or deadlines.

The list is endless. But the aforementioned examples will give you a flavor of the challenges in creating Customer Value across a wide field, from consumer products to state-provided services.

There are more examples of Customer Value Starvation, or even Destruction, than of Creation. But we cannot sit back and watch the downslide. We need to do the best we can to prevent Customer Value Starvation.

Innovation Is the Key to Avoid the Stage of Customer Value Starvation

It is always said that prevention is better than cure. Rather than maintaining a *satisfactory stage* by just about avoiding Customer Value Starvation, it is better to keep thinking how you can increase customer satisfaction, even though things are going well at present. It is like building refrigerated warehouses for farm crops, so that in the nonproduction period, there will always be a good and free-flow supply. Customers then do not look for alternatives!

Companies with great success and no long-term vision will, over time, be defeated and vanish. There are too many examples of these even in recent times. There was Kodak, a household name and a virtual monopoly; there was BlackBerry, another household name; there was Pierre Cardin and many others. Where are they now? They are all victims of innovation—innovation managed by competition. In most cases, it is also the Davids who then killed the Goliaths.

The basic directive principle never fails: Keep improving the Product, Process, Price offering, Distribution, and Service—all, one, or some, at any one time. If you don't, someone else will, and make you obsolete.

That is how most of the Davids in India became Goliaths.

There was a washing powder company, Nirma that unseated Unilever as the virtual monopoly in this market. Nirma offered lower, but acceptable, quality at a lower price, which was attractive because the target user was the lower class or the domestic help of the upper class. Nirma created mass awareness, and it paid off. By the time Unilever realized what was happening, Nirma had become a respected competitor, to a well-established multinational.

There was Rasna, fruit juice powder for the first time in India. It pushed aside well-established brands like Rex and Kissan into a corner.

These were liquids in a bottle, which meant breakages, high freight, and much higher price. Rasna became a convenient and cheaper substitute.

There was Velvette shampoo, packed in single-use sachets and therefore available at a very low price. It shook the foundations of large sales created by multinationals for their brands, over many decades. These were far more expensive in large bottles and with fancy packaging. In a few years they all had to follow suit.

In a reverse, Coca-Cola showed the way to anticipate customer needs and fulfil them. It had the slogan, "Drink Coca-Cola, ice cold." But this was not possible in remote areas of India where there is no electricity. So Coke developed a solar-powered icebox, for storage *only* of Coke, and distributed it to the dealers. In the remotest parts now, Coke can be had ice cold!

All these companies looked at satisfied customers and found out how they could be further satisfied. In the process, with their new offering, customers felt they were starved by their earlier providers of a similar product/service.

Of course, it would have been better if the same company reinvented its products continuously every few years and therefore remained in the forefront. But it is never easy because the larger a company becomes, the faster it forgets the very lessons that made it successful.

Ongoing innovation is the key to avoid the stage of Customer Value Starvation—easier said than done!

What a Pleasant Surprise

An article written by Walter in 1997 titled "What a Pleasant Surprise" is reproduced here. Walter remembers the Customer Value Creation.

The excitement of getting an unexpected gift will undoubtedly bring in lots of goodwill, which will work miracles for corporates. Most people like to receive something free, especially when they do not expect it. It comes as a pleasant surprise. Most people are also touched by a positive comment on their personality or their future. Marketers have always looked for ways and means in which to put these two "soft spots" to use, the Achilles' heel, so to say, in the human psyche.

When you arrive at Bali in Indonesia anytime of the day or night, two young Balinese ladies greet you at the airport terminal exit. One gives you a map of Bali and another gives you a sun shade. Both give all arriving tourists a broad and sincere smile. It makes tourists to Bali feel welcome and sets the right tone for a relaxed holiday after a long flight.

Closer home, we have those arriving in Bangalore Airport, being greeted at the exit by young ladies presenting each traveler with a large red rose. "Welcome to Bangalore, the garden city" and with the complements of Kids Kemp, the world's largest store for children's garments. This claim may or may not be true. But the goodwill has been generated with the presentation of the red rose. And if and when the visitor to Bangalore actually does go to Kids Kemp to do some shopping whether the "window" or "actual" kind, the staff at Kids Kemp will insist you have a cool drink and the children have sweets or chewing gum—all "on the house" and with no obligation. They spread goodwill and cheer. And which visitor will be stonehearted as to walk out without even buying a pair of socks?

It was the late-lamented Damania Airways that began cultivating airline travelers and delighted them with the offer, "Show your boarding card at the cafeteria and you can get a coffee, tea or soft drink on the house." Indian Airlines offered this service only to business class travelers. Damania Airlines (now defunct) offered this to everyone. They made a ceremony of it by issuing a separate card to be presented at the cafeteria that would entitle you to a free coffee. Damania simplified it and made it easy and without *formality*. The customer was delighted, and Damania generated immense goodwill.

Walking around the stalls at the annual textile exhibition "Intestoffe" at Frankfurt can be a great education. There are the stalls of the Italian manufacturers, some of whom will serve Italian wine to all prospects who visit the stall. Visitors are made to feel welcome, relaxed before they talk business. There are the Turkish textile stalls that serve Turkish coffee, steaming and strong, in dainty coffee cups. There are the Indian textile stalls that keep cashew nuts and some other dry fruits, closely guarded under the counter and only brought out when those manning the stall have been able to distinguish between those who are really prospects and those who may only be *suspects*. Sometimes this causes a piquant, even uproariously funny, situation as the tray is first brought out, and then, hastily pushed back in!

At the Mandarin restaurant in Mumbai, the paper table mats give an illustrated example of the lines of the hand and how they can be interpreted. The mat kept us busy and amused as all of us kept comparing the lines on our own hands with those on the mat and then looking for the explanations given. It gave us something to talk about and something to laugh about. It sets the right mood for a good meal. There was laughter and good cheer and I suppose it created indirectly, as a spillover, some goodwill for the Mandarin restaurant.

At the China Garden restaurant in Mumbai, the paper table mats have a horoscope guide according to the Chinese system. At the dinner I attended with nine others, we spent nearly half an hour on figuring out where each of us belonged. A quick calculation had to be done. Was it the year of the rat or the year of the horse? And then the horoscope was read. Strange, that these horoscopes generally project a glorious future rather than a gloomy one. But we believe what we like to believe!

It was only the prodding of the steward that pushed us into quickly placing our orders for the meal. But the interest in the table mat was abiding. Many of us took the mat home after the meal. China Garden probably also intended it to be so. It creates goodwill for the restaurant.

There are other Chinese restaurants, like Ling's Pavilion in the city, that will serve a plateful of fortune cookies at the end of the meal when they bring the check. Inside the dry chocolate crust is a little piece of paper that gives you a personal message. "The next 6-month period will be full of romantic encounters. You will have to be careful." Yes, there is an admonition, but you would like to believe this, and with this parting shot, you leave the pleasant environs of Ling's Pavilion.

As a schoolboy it gave me great pleasure to check my weight at the weight machine every few months. My friends did the same. The attraction was not the indication of the weight that appears on one side of the card, but the other side of the card that gave some pleasant prediction. The weight machines created great interest in us. It gave us the pleasure of getting the unexpected.

Also, in the case of the placard announcing our names at Goa airport as we walked out. Who was this and why? It was the hotel where we had booked our rooms. They had sent a car to the airport to fetch us. It was a complimentary service. We saved Rs. 550 on the regular taxi hire. But it was more. It was the pleasure of being offered the unexpected, pleasant surprise!

Avoid Customer Value Starvation with Relationship Marketing

So many ways to avoid Customer Value Starvation. Everyone from the chairman to the doorman has to use concern, creativity, and empathy, again and again, to retain the customer.

I have mostly been unlucky with relationship managers who have been assigned to my account, by my banks. This has been the pattern for many years. I have had relationship managers managing my mutual fund investments. I am unsure if they recommend funds where the bank gets a better commission rather than where the investor gets the best returns. When questioned he or she will tell me that the fund I am recommending as a possibility is either unsafe or it does not have enough number of years of continuous success or it is not on their list of well-researched mutual funds. The relationship manager will be oblivious to the fact that some of your mutual funds are earning a return of 1 percent for the last 2 years. Does he point this out and suggest a pull out and reinvestment in another mutual fund giving higher returns or even put into fixed deposits, which will give a higher return, even after taxes? No, he is oblivious to the goings on in my account.

Before I know what has happened, the relationship manager has left the bank and moved elsewhere for better prospects and I have to go through a whole period of initiation with a new relationship manager, who, I am certain, will follow the same pattern. It may have been better not to have had a relationship manager or just call him a "contact manager" rather than having to change the definition of "relationship," which is intended to create *good, warm, and mutually beneficial relationships.*

But as a goodwill gesture of the bank, he or she will send a nice diary to a "privileged customer" at mid/end January, when a busy and privileged customer is already using a diary purchased by him at end November of the previous year.

You can call relationship marketing what you want. Give it any label. The essence is that it is a simple secret that can be used by anyone who *devotes time and talent to serve the customer*!

Customer Rage

by
Marc Grainer, Scott M. Broetzmann, and David Beinhacker

We thought we could share the Customer Rage study conducted in the United States. The ACSI (American Customer Satisfaction Index) score has not changed much over the years. Why? The ACSI is 76 percent today versus 75 percent in the 1990s.

National ACSI Score
Baseline 1994 to Q2 2019
(0-100 Scale)

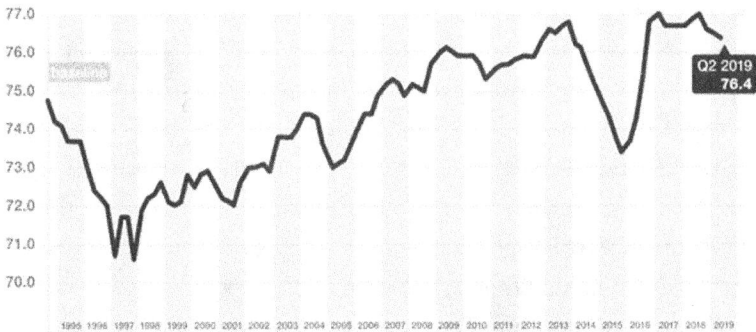

Another factor to consider is customer rage. Sensationalized stories about customer rage are reported by the media on a regular basis. Whether road rage or upset passengers on airplanes, it is safe to say that rage today is worse than in the mid-1970s. Results from the 2003–2013 surveys illustrate just how pervasive this phenomenon has become. Sixty-eight percent of the respondents to these surveys experienced rage ("extremely" or "very upset") in connection with their most serious product/service problem. For the majority of those households experiencing problems, then, rage has become a significant issue in the new millennium.

The Customer Rage Studies report evidence of a negative relationship between complainant satisfaction and rage. Eighty-two percent of the problems reported by dissatisfied complainers caused customer rage. On the other hand, only 60 percent of those problems reported by satisfied complainants caused rage, a drop of 22 percentage points.

These data suggest that it may be more difficult to satisfy complainants who have experienced rage. This rage may be acting to mitigate corporate efforts to satisfy complainants. The bad news is that there is little prospect that the level of customer rage will decrease anytime soon.

Changing Customer Expectations

Customer expectations are another factor that has an influence on complainant satisfaction. Such expectations are not static. What was acceptable in the mid-1970s may no longer measure up to today's higher expectations.

Given business's generally negative attitude toward handling complaints in the mid-1970s, it is safe to assume that most customers expected relatively little when they complained. When the White House Study was conducted, responding to a complaint letter within weeks may have been an acceptable norm. On the other hand, in the age of the Internet, the expected response time for a complaint submitted via e-mail may be within minutes/hours.

It's not just the consumer movement that has raised customer expectations. Business can also claim much of the credit. Companies contribute to this escalation in expectations by overstressing the reliability of their offerings through unrealistic advertising messages or by promising 100 percent satisfaction. Therefore, although business has upgraded its efforts to facilitate the submission and resolution of complaints, these initiatives may not be keeping up with today's rising customer expectations.

The Nature of Today's Customer Problems

Today's customer problems are different and more difficult to resolve than those in the past.

In 2013, 5 out of the 10 products/services that caused the most problems (cable/satellite television, cell phones, consumer electronics [non-computer], computer services [e.g., Internet providers], and computer equipment) hardly existed in the 1970s. Resolving complaints about these products/services is much more difficult than handling complaints dealing with such top- tier problem types from the White House Study as mail service, clothing, or food.

While both the telephone and automobiles were among the product types that caused the most problems in both studies, there is a substantial difference between these products today and in 1976. Telephones from the 1970s were quite simple instruments, while today most offer a wide range of sophisticated functionality (caller ID, call waiting, voice mail, e-mail, a myriad of apps, etc.). Automobiles from the twenty-first century, likewise, offer a wide range of new features (GPS, entertainment systems, multiple computers for operations and diagnostics, etc.). The upgraded complexity of these products, then, can add to the difficulty of satisfying complainants.

Companies Do All the Right Things the Wrong Way

The problem with the *upgraded* complaint-handling practices initiated by business during the last 30-plus years may not be one of adopting the wrong programs but, instead, may be poor execution.

Customer care call centers provide a good example of this point. All too often, when customers attempt to contact such centers, they're put on hold for unreasonably long periods, can't easily navigate confusing automated response systems, aren't able to reach a live agent when necessary, and, if they do reach a live body, the agent may not be empowered to act on the complainant's problem.

When run ineffectively, such call centers can be the subject of double customer rage. First, the customer is upset about the problem, which is the reason for the call. Second, even if the problem is ultimately solved, the pain suffered in contacting the call center may engender an additional bout of rage.

This scenario has become so much of a cliché that some companies have actually designed major advertising campaigns that satirize the poor call center service offered by their competitors (e.g., Discover Card's "Peggy" television ads).

Another recent example concerns a major airline that experienced significant delays answering customer calls as a result of restructuring its customer care call centers. This problem was so severe that it e-mailed an apology for the poor service to its *premium-level* frequent fliers, regardless of whether these customers had actually tried to contact the airline.

The problem doesn't lie with the use of call centers per se. On the contrary, going back as far as the White House Study in the 1970s, those centers that were run effectively both satisfied a high percentage of complainants and earned positive ROIs. On the other hand, ineffectively managed centers generally reported low levels of complainant satisfaction and returned negative ROIs.

In sum, it's probably more of an issue of poor implementation than the inherent nature of the customer care initiatives adopted by business that has had the biggest negative impact on complainant satisfaction. If this is the case, a good rule of thumb for business would be to Do It Right, Or Don't Do It.

So What, Why Should Business Care about Upgrading Its Customer Complaint–Handling Practices?

There are two marketing-related reasons why business should care: (1) the retention of existing customers and (2) conquest sales to new customers.

First, extrapolating from the 2013 Customer Rage Study data to the U.S. population as a whole, 56,000,000 households experienced at least one product/service-related problem during the 12 months preceding the survey (% of problem incidence × number of U.S. households). This translates into an eye-popping revenue at risk to business of $75,992,000,000 (number of households experiencing at least one product/service problem during the 12 months preceding the survey × the mean cost of those products/services that caused these households' most serious customer problems). Given today's low levels of complainant satisfaction (and the *bupkis*/double *bupkis* phenomenon), much of this revenue is not being recovered by business.

The revenue at risk calculated here only applies to households' most serious problems. When households' less serious problems are considered, the total yearly revenue at risk would be substantially higher.

Second, one of the most effective marketing tools available to business for winning new customers is word-of-mouth communication to friends, neighbors, relatives, and so on. In the 2013 Customer Rage Study, households reporting problems told an average of 19.2 people about their experience. Again, given the low levels of complainant satisfaction, most of these communications were negative. (Sixty percent of the word-of-mouth communication reported by complainants in the 2007–2013 Customer Rage Studies was negative.) With the advent of posting on the Internet, one person can now reach many thousands or more with a few keystrokes.

In sum, those businesses that don't handle complaints effectively put their market share at significant risk. They stand to lose both existing and future customers.

This does not mean that business should give in to unreasonable customer demands. On the contrary, business should always do a cost–benefit analysis, where the cost of the remedy is balanced against the value of the customer's future patronage/word-of-mouth communication. If there is nothing that can be done to save the unhappy customers' future patronage or to mitigate their negative word of mouth, the value of the remedy offered should be minimized. However, because the demands of most complainants are reasonable, a complaint-based marketing strategy can be quite successful.

A Road Map for Increasing Complainant Satisfaction

Although the Customer Rage Studies have well documented the aggregate poor performance of business to satisfy complainants, there is some cause for optimism. A road map does exist for improved complainant satisfaction, and these recommendations will cost business little, and in some cases will actually save money. This road map of best practices consists of six sets of recommendations.

1. Proper Use of the Telephone

CCMC's 2013 Customer Rage Study reported 67 percent of complainants using the telephone as their primary channel for complaining. Therefore, a key to improving satisfaction rests with the proper use of the telephone to handle complaints.

The 2005/2006 Conventional Wisdom Study cataloged the telephone complaint–handling practices that customers liked and disliked. Using a 0 to 10 point scale (where "10" meant "Would Significantly Increase Your Satisfaction" and "0" meant "Would Significantly Decrease Your Satisfaction"), a sample of customers, who had submitted telephone complaints about product/service problems during the preceding year, rated the influence of 85 complaint-handling practices on their satisfaction. The objective of this study was to determine the validity of those assumptions that are the basis for contemporary complaint–handling practice.[iii]

Scores from this study that were 2.50 and below are considered to be strongly negative. Five sets of complaint-handling practices that fall into this negative territory bear special mention.

First, many call centers that handle complaints try to piggyback sales campaigns onto their response to customer problems. The thought is that, once the company has the customer on the telephone, it's possible to *kill two birds with one stone.*

While from a productivity standpoint such practices may seem to make sense, the findings from the Conventional Wisdom Study argue strongly against mixing sales efforts with complaint handling. Selling after resolving the problem (1.58), selling before resolving the problem (1.23), and continuing to sell after being told "no" (1.01) were among those complaint-handling practices that caused the most dissatisfaction.

Second, telephone technology was another area that caused dissatisfaction. Examples of such practices were "when they transfer you to another department, you have to use an automated telephone system before you talk with an agent" (2.43), "you're told how to reach a person only after you've had to listen to a long message" (2.15), and "when you must use an automated telephone system, there's no option to talk to a person" (1.19). Complainant satisfaction suffers when companies make it difficult to talk to live agents.

Third, agent response practices like talking too fast and an inability to understand agents because of their accents received strongly negative ratings of 2.38 and 1.98, respectively.

The speed problem is often as a result of setting unrealistically high agent call-handling quotas. When this is the case, the data suggest that quality is more important than quantity. Handling fewer calls well is better than closing more calls badly. Productivity at the cost of complainant satisfaction will rarely translate into increased brand loyalty.

Accent is a more complex issue. In some cases, accent can impede understanding. Failure to successfully communicate with customers makes it difficult to resolve their complaints. Accent can also suggest outsourcing outside the United States, another significant cause of dissatisfaction.

While training can sometimes improve agent response practices (proper greetings, anger diffusion techniques, etc.), speed and accent problems are more often the result of strategic call center policies, not a deficiency in the agent skills. In this instance, misplaced productivity and cost concerns can result in lower complainant satisfaction.

Fourth, on the basis of anecdotal data, one of the most maddening customer care practices is having to repeat information that has already been provided. This ranges from customers having to repeat long numeric ID numbers to being asked to restate the reason why they're calling. In this instance, the anecdotal data mirrors Conventional Wisdom Study results. Having to repeat information received a strongly negative score of 2.15.

Basic case-tracking software should preclude the need to repeat case-related information when the caller is transferred to a second agent or when the customer makes a follow-up call. Numeric IDs are often used to access information from the company's customer database. If these links are in place, customers should not have to be asked for their numeric ID twice. Most modern call centers, then, should not need to ask their customers to unnecessarily repeat information.

Fifth, as would be expected, remedy has the greatest impact on complainant satisfaction. Getting "none of the things you ask for" received the lowest score of the 85 complaint-handling practices that were being rated, a strong negative score of 0.66.

In the real world, of course, resolution of customer complaints is not necessarily an all or nothing proposition. While it may not be feasible to give complainants everything they want, it is generally possible to give complaining customers something (partial monetary compensation, an apology, an opportunity to vent, etc.). Getting partial resolution to the customers' problems scored 3.55. Although, still a negative rating, this complaint-handling practice received a score more than five times higher than giving complainants nothing.

Scores from the Conventional Wisdom Study of 7.50 and above are considered to be strongly positive. These customer preferences covered a wide range of complaint-handling practices.

The positive side of remedy ("you get everything you ask for") has the strongest influence on satisfying complainants. This received a score of 8.92, the highest rating given to any of the 85 telephone complaint–handling practices.

Agent response practices also strongly influence complainant satisfaction. Follow through on promises (8.91), agent knowledge (8.85), courtesy (8.72), empowerment (8.65), 24/7 agent availability (8.63), use of plain English (8.43), and agents telling complainants their names (7.87) all scored in the strongly positive range.

Ease of finding the number to call in order to reach the offending company is another strong positive influence of complainant satisfaction. Putting the number on the product, on the bill, product packaging, and product advertising all received scores above 7.50.

Other telephone practices that received strong positive scores included being given a unique case reference number if there is a need to call back (8.15), timeliness of response (8.55), being told how long it will take to resolve the complaint (8.34), being able to contact the same agent if the complaint can't be resolved in one contact (7.76), and, when the call is initially answered by an automated response system, being given the option to talk to a live agent at the beginning of the instructions (7.87).

Recommendation: The Conventional Wisdom Study identified 16 strongly negative and 27 strongly positive telephone complaint–handling practices. Whenever possible, companies should avoid these negative practices and adopt the positive ones.

2. First Contact Resolution/Ping-ponging

One of the key metrics used to assess corporate complaint–handling practices is the rate of first contact resolution. The White House Study found that 33 percent of complainants made only one contact to the place where the offending product/service was purchased. Thirty-plus years later, the rate of first contact resolution as reported by the 2003–2013 Customer Rage Studies has dropped to 20 percent.

The importance of first contact resolution is recognized by the Conventional Wisdom Study. This complaint-handling practice rated fourth out of the 85 telephone practices being assessed, with a score of 8.81.

All things being equal, the fewer contacts complainants need to make to resolve their problems, the higher the level of satisfaction. The 2003–2013 Customer Rage Studies reported substantial drops in complainant satisfaction when the customer found it necessary to make multiple contacts. There was a drop from 60 percent complainant satisfaction for one contact to 48 percent when two contacts were required. Only 34 percent of complainants were satisfied when three or more contacts were reported.

The irony for business is that the greater the number of contacts, the higher the administrative cost incurred and the more monetary remedy that is needed to resolve the complainant's problem. Therefore, many businesses are spending the bulk of their complaint-handling budgets on those customers who are the least satisfied, who will be the least brand loyal in the future, and who are responsible for the most negative word of mouth.

A somewhat more sensitive metric is ping-ponging (the average number of contacts needed to resolve a complaint). This metric better takes into account any skew toward multiple contacts. Here again the average ping-ponging rate reported by the White House Study (3.5) is lower than that found 30-plus years later by the Customer Rage Studies (4.1).

Recommendation: In order to improve complainant satisfaction, business should increase first contact resolution and decrease the rate of ping-ponging: First contact resolution targets should be above 50 percent; ping-pong rates should be below 1.5. (Of course, companies that handle complex complaints dealing with expensive products/services will generally score worse on these metrics than businesses handling simple problems with small ticket items.)

The trick to improving performance on such metrics is to assign realistic improvement targets and let management formulate product/company-specific policies designed to achieve these objectives. The key is tailoring the remedial policies to fit every company's unique needs.

3. The Power of Nonmonetary Remedies

Data from the 2004–2013 Customer Rage Studies report an intriguing relationship between the type of remedy received and complainant satisfaction.[iv] Not surprisingly, those who felt they got only nonmonetary remedies reported the lowest level of satisfaction (21 percent). Those who received only monetary remedies nearly doubled their level of complainant satisfaction to 37 percent. What is more interesting, though, is the satisfaction uplift reported by complainants who got both monetary and nonmonetary remedies. Here the level of complainant satisfaction increased to 74 percent.

Providing both monetary and nonmonetary remedies, then, recognizes that to resolve customer complaints, business must deal with both fixing the offending product/service problems and with addressing customer emotions. Best practice is to use apologies, opportunities to vent, and so on to defuse customer rage. Use of such techniques can significantly shorten the staff time required to handle especially difficult problems, thereby decreasing personnel costs.

Recommendation: Whenever feasible, business should offer complainants both monetary and nonmonetary relief. This approach may mitigate the extent of the double *bupkis* phenomenon.

4. Outsourcing

Outsourcing the handling of customer complaints has been a growing trend over the last two decades. The logic for this policy is twofold.

First, companies outsource as a cost containment strategy. Outsourcing agencies argue that they offer savings on personnel, facilities, technology, and so on.

Second, the trend in recent years has been for business to concentrate on core competencies. Most companies do not have a core competency in best practice complaint handling. This is most often the case in areas such as customer care personnel and telephone technology. The argument, then, is that outsourcing agencies can offer higher quality complaint-handling services.

While school is still out on the validity of these rationales, the Conventional Wisdom Study provides a complainant perspective on outsourcing. Here the reaction to outsourcing was decidedly negative. Outsourcing outside the United States received a strong negative rating for both telephone (2.01) and e-mail (2.17) complaint handling. Even the general concept of outsourcing ("using an outside agency to answer your complaint") was viewed negatively (a 3.29 score for telephone and 3.08 for e-mail complaints).

Evidence that business has begun to recognize the marketing disadvantages of outsourcing overseas is found in a Consumer Cellular television ad campaign. These ads stress the fact that Consumer Cellular's products come "with great customer support, right here in the United States." Further, most of the automobile companies that outsourced overseas have brought their call centers back to the United States.

The savings from outsourcing overseas are largely based on the low personnel costs in these international complaint–handling centers. Such savings, however, can be illusory.

For example, international centers often have higher ping-pong rates. (More customer call backs are required to resolve the product/service problem than would be the case in a comparable U.S. center.) Because companies are typically charged by the call, not the case, the true cost of resolving the customer's complaint may be camouflaged.

Done correctly, outsourcing should be transparent to the complainant. When transparent, these negative feelings toward outsourcing should not be a cause of complainant dissatisfaction.

Unfortunately, transparency is all often not the case. Accent, lack of product/service knowledge, incorrect grammar, lack of empowerment are examples of the factors that may suggest to complainants that their problems are being handled by outsourcing agencies.

When Ford first established its complaint-handling call center, it used this center as a training ground for new hires who would ultimately be assigned to other departments (e.g., the field organization) of the company. This year to 2-year assignment created a cadre of future executives who had been sensitized to customer needs. When Ford outsourced its call center function, this on-the-job training vehicle was lost.

Recommendation: Before deciding to outsource the complaint-handling function, business must weigh any of the potential benefits against complainants' negative attitudes toward this policy. If the decision is to outsource, this doesn't mean that a company should wash its hands of any complaint-handling responsibility. On the contrary, management oversight of the outsourcing agency is extremely important. Formulating response rules, content of training programs, timely provision of remedies, and satisfaction surveys are among those areas where providing such oversight is critical.

5. Satisfaction Surveys

Satisfaction surveys of complainants have become a standard tool for evaluating the performance of customer care agents, administrative support systems (e.g., telephone technology), and response rules. Used correctly, data gleaned from such surveys can serve as an important management tool.

The Conventional Wisdom Study addressed what impact fielding these surveys had on complainant satisfaction. The results from this study provided a mixed set of reviews.

For telephone complaints, asking the complainant "if you are satisfied with (the) response before ending the call" (6.60) and "they ask you to take a satisfaction survey a few days or weeks after you've called for help" (5.70) had a positive influence on complainant satisfaction. Survey practices that had a more negative impact on satisfaction included, "you're invited to take a satisfaction survey at the end of the call, using an automated telephone system" (4.33), "they encourage you to say you're completely satisfied if you receive a satisfaction survey" (3.83), and "they don't address your concerns after you use a survey to tell them you're dissatisfied" (1.62).

Similar findings were reported for e-mail complainants. While being requested to participate in a survey (5.06) had a neutral impact on complainant satisfaction, being coached (asking complainants to respond that they are completely satisfied) and not addressing problems raised in responses to a survey had negative (3.80) and strongly negative (1.45) impacts, respectively, on satisfaction.

On occasion, satisfaction surveys may be designed in ways that measure complainant satisfaction incompletely. For example, surveys administered at the end of a complaint call are effective tools for assessing agent performance but don't measure the impact of monetary remedies that are to be delivered in the future. (e.g., it may be days after the call is completed before it is possible to determine whether the defective product has been fixed) Both process and outcome measures are necessary to accurately gauge the level of complainant satisfaction.

In other instances, survey instrumentation may be a problem (e.g., use scales that are biased toward the positive). Such surveys can be designed to produce high scores and not accurately measure performance. This most often happens when complainant satisfaction is tied to financial incentives.

Finally, some surveys try to measure too much. As a result of asking too many questions and not focusing on those relatively few items that are the key drivers of complainant satisfaction, management may direct remedial action toward improving performance in low-scoring areas that have little influence on satisfaction.

Recommendation: When fielding satisfaction surveys, business should refrain from coaching complainants and respond to any problems raised by returned questionnaires. Further, basic rules of survey design should be followed in order to accurately measure complainant satisfaction.

6. The Internet as a Channel for Complaining

The Customer Rage Studies reported that the Internet is still not a major channel for complaining. Only 4 percent of complainants designated the web as their primary channel for complaining in 2003. Internet usage for complaining had only increased to 7 percent by 2013. While the trend is upward, the Internet is still no match for the telephone as the primary channel most customers use for submitting complaints to business.

When the effectiveness of Internet and telephone complaint–handling practices was compared, in terms of complainant satisfaction, there was not a much of a difference. Forty-three percent of telephone versus 41 percent of Internet complainers were satisfied.

Next, the 2011 Customer Rage Study included two sets of questions that focused solely on Internet usage.

First, complainants were asked whether they had posted information about their most serious problem on any of four specified types of websites (the offending company's site, social networking sites, social media sites, and/or sites that review products/services). Twenty-seven percent had posted on at least one of these sites. By 2013, this percentage had escalated to 45 percent. While not complaining behavior per se, these postings often contain information about the complaining experience.

When asked why they posted on these sites, more than half of the reasons given related to deterring others from having similar bad experiences. This suggests that business should be concerned about the potential of market damage resulting from such postings.

Second, the study found that Internet users can be quite discerning interpreters of the information they receive via the web. When social networking[v] users were asked whether postings about good or bad experiences with products/services had the most influence on their future purchasing decisions, good experiences were designated as most influential by a margin of more than two to one (46 percent to 19 percent). Further, by a margin of 53 to 33 percent these respondents were more likely to post information about good as opposed to bad experiences.

Recommendation: While the use of the Internet for complaining is increasing, it would be a mistake for business to disproportionately invest in this channel. This is especially true given the fact that complaining via the web provides no advantage in complainant satisfaction.

Forcing customers to use the web may be a shortsighted policy. Business should be concerned that any cost savings resulting from channeling complainants to the web may be offset by the increased dissatisfaction of customers who prefer to use other channels to complain. Customers should be allowed to use the channels of their choice.

This has been the approach adopted by Esurance. Although this insurance company's business model stresses use of the Internet, the theme of its advertising campaigns has been that the customer has a choice of channels: "People when you want them, technology when you don't." The tagline to its marketing campaign has been "Insurance for the modern world, click or call."

While the web still may not be the primary channel for submitting complaints, the 2011 Customer Rage Study does find that postings about customer problems reach a wide audience. To date, much of business's concern has focused on deterring/removing negative postings. The 2011 survey, however, suggests that these efforts may be somewhat misplaced. Instead, the data suggest that a higher priority should be given to promoting the posting of positive experiences. Upgraded complaint-handling practices can be an effective means for increasing such positive postings.

The Bottom-Line Implications of These Recommendations

If these recommendations are adopted by business, it is not unreasonable to project an aggregate national increase of 10 to15 percentage points in complainant satisfaction. Given the relationship between satisfaction and brand loyalty reported by the Customer Rage Studies, this should lead to the incremental retention of billions of dollars' worth of sales that otherwise would have been lost. Further, there would be additional sales made to new customers due to the increase in positive word-of-mouth communication resulting from more satisfied complainants.

Conclusion

The White House Study from the mid-1970s found a positive relationship between complaining and brand loyalty. On the basis of this finding, the U.S. Office of Consumer Affairs advised business to increase investment in corporate complaint–handling practices.

The argument was that soliciting complaints would result in an uplift in brand loyalty even if customer problems were not satisfactorily resolved. Satisfying complaints would result in an even higher uplift in brand loyalty. This would allow business to retain billions of dollars of sales that otherwise would have been lost. The increased positive word-of-mouth communication resulting from satisfying complainants would be an added marketing plus. Over the last 30-plus years, business has bought into this argument and has invested heavily in upgraded complaint-handling programs.

The Customer Rage Studies (2003–2013) found a somewhat mitigated relationship between complaining and brand loyalty. It now only pays to solicit complaints if the customer ends up being satisfied.

The good news, however, was that satisfying complainants still resulted in enough increased incremental brand loyalty to form the basis of a meaningful retention marketing strategy. The bad news was that the early promise of upgraded complaint-handling practices remains largely unfulfilled. The investment in expanded corporate programs has not paid off in increased complainant satisfaction. On the contrary, satisfaction has actually decreased over the past 30-plus years.

Complainant satisfaction has not increased because of both external and internal factors.

External factors like rising customer expectations and the more complex products/services that dominate today's marketplace probably have contributed to the depressed levels of satisfaction. The same holds true with the escalating customer rage that characterizes society today. On the internal front, business's miserly provision of remedies (*bupkis* and double *bupkis*) certainly has not been a policy designed to improve satisfaction.

The primary reason satisfaction has not increased is that, all too often, companies *do all the right things, the wrong way*. The programs being utilized by business to handle complaints are basically sound. The fault lies less with these programs but more with issues of poor execution.

Findings from the Customer Rage and Conventional Wisdom Studies do, however, provide some basis for optimism. A road map of six recommendations is proposed, which, if adopted, could improve aggregate national complainant satisfaction by 10 to 15 percentage points. Implementing these recommendations would cost business little or nothing. In fact, some probably would save business money (e.g., decreased ping-ponging).

It should be possible to retain billions of dollars of future sales that business might otherwise have lost. This optimism is based on the premise that only by improving *performance* will the original promise of upgraded corporate complaint-handling practices ever be fulfilled.

Value Starvation and Ethics

Many companies resort to unethical practices, or questionable practices, but kid themselves (and try to kid the public) that they are doing something to improve business. One such example is Volkswagen, which fudged emissions data.

VW has been in the news as its chiefs, CEO Diess, Chairman Poetsch, and former CEO Winterkorn, were charged criminally for withholding information on poor emissions and cheating. Possible market manipulating is alleged and the US SEC (Securities and Exchange Commission) is also suing on similar charges. It was 4 years ago that the US EPA stated that VW had been selling vehicles that polluted more than allowable limits. This scandal is now known as Dieselgate.

The cheating happened because VW had installed software that showed reduced emissions when tested. The pollution levels were 40 times more than allowable and 11 million vehicles were involved. What a massive fraud.

Fines and other payments of over $30 billion were made, and many executives were charged, fired, or arrested. Worse still the European Union has charged VW with colluding with Daimler and BMW! BMW is being investigated in the United States.

Poor ethics is Customer Value Starvation and can also lead to Value Deprivation and Value Destruction!

Boeing tried to hide a design flaw problem on the 737Max. This design flaw was linked to two fatal crashes, in Indonesia and Ethiopia. This is a case of flawed ethics. It is almost like the famous Ford Pinto case, where a flawed fuel system could cause a fire. Ford looked at the cost–benefit–risk analysis and concluded it was cheaper to compensate for possible deaths than to fix the problem and avoid injury or death. Is this ethical?

They might or might not lose customers, depending on what the most important reasons to trust the company are. If making good cars, giving good service is, and emissions are low on the list, then loss of customers may be low. But for those customers for whom emissions, ecology, and sustainability are important, there is a grievous breach of trust.

J&J Soap/Shampoo Story

For many of us, children were brought up using Johnson's baby soap, powder, and shampoo. These products have now come under the scanner, and the powder is looked at suspiciously because "it contains asbestos." J&J denies this.

But J&J's integrity is being questioned because of large gaps in expectations and results in another, totally unrelated area—hip implants.

The apex child rights body in India has asked all states to stop sale of Johnson's baby shampoo after its sample was found to be of substandard quality in a lab test.

In a letter to chief secretaries of all states, April 2019, the, the National Commission for Protection of Child Rights (NCPCR) ordered stoppage of sale of Johnson's baby shampoo and also removing the product from stocks of shops after the Drug Testing Laboratory, Jaipur, declared it of substandard quality, as the presence of formaldehyde was confirmed in it.

The apex child rights body had sought sample test reports of Johnson's baby shampoo and talcum powder from authorities of five states—Andhra Pradesh (south), Jharkhand (east), Rajasthan (west), Madhya Pradesh (central), and Assam (northeast)—after reports of the presence of asbestos and carcinogenic substance in them emerged.

The order to stop sale was issued after test reports of the baby shampoo sample from Rajasthan came in. It is yet to receive the test reports from the other four states.

It has asked the drug control officer of Rajasthan to send the test report of the talcum powder at the earliest.

J&J Told to Pay Rs 1 Crore Compensation to Faulty Hip Transplant Patient

- The R. K. Arya Committee had examined the case's documents to decide on compensation
- The developments came months after the newspaper Mint investigation exposed the plight of patients who had suffered due to faulty implants

How Cheats Get Away at the Expense of Honest Citizens

There are people who cheat and are allowed to get away with. In Delhi many store owners have used illegal structures and illegal basements for years. Now the Supreme Court has mandated that these illegal structures should be sealed. These owners are up in arms. If they get away with it, it will mean Value Starvation for honest people and honest taxpayers.

One of the finest and most concise articles I have read on ethics in business and corporate leadership was written by Jayanta Roy in the *Times of India* in January 2020 (https://ift.tt/2tJk2Yo).

He states that ethical choices employees make can influence leaders' ethical choices. He also finds that ethical organizations have a higher retention rate than nonethical ones; they have more customer loyalty and productivity. We always state Values create Value, and Tata is an example.

Ethics, according to him, builds trust and trust builds business. Doing business with integrity matters. Remember the employer's or the leader's ethics is as important, if not more important, than the employee's ethics.

Walter's comment: We have a long list of CEOs of companies who have thrown ethics to the winds. The list is large and keeps growing.

We have referred to the CEOs of BMW and Volkswagen, of Toyota and J&J. Even the President of South Korea had to resign recently because the reports that she had accepted bribes from Samsung were proved correct.

The list of bank defaulters in India continues to grow. There were large amounts due from Vijay Mallya and Lalit Modi earlier, but some of the later ones, like ILFS, showed how large defaults can really be. At last count, the total dues to the banks were estimated to be Rs 7 lakh crores! Many of the defaulters are abroad, from London to St. Kitts. Some of them had no time to escape and are still held up in India. The latest is the CEO of YES Bank. He provided customer value to clients who were not credit worthy, while at the same time, siphoning off funds to his own large number of shell companies. And clients of the bank (and of PMC Bank a little earlier) keep wondering whether all their life's savings will just have to be written off. That is Customer Value Starvation, bordering on Customer Value Destruction.

Learnings from Value Creation—Four Types of Companies

I have learned from my experience with creating value and watching people and businesses around me, just as many of you have learned from your experiences. Do relate what follows to what you have noticed in your life. This reflection will help you look at businesses in a different light.

Lewis Hyde's book *The Gift* suggests that the most unbelievable gift is one with no expectations of a return, and is truly unexpected. Value Creation is all about giving, not just taking. And delight occurs when you are given an unexpected experience!

The concept of Giving and just not Taking is embedded in the New Purpose of a Company.

There are four types of people and companies:

1. True Givers, Altruistic: These are people who give selflessly. They do so without any expectation of a return or what this will mean for them. I have been lucky in my journey to come across many such givers. You go to such people for help and they go out of their way to help, without asking unnecessary questions. They are true Value Creators. Many parents, teachers, and social workers give selflessly. I have true friends who fall into this category.

Examples of this from the world of business are Azim Premji of Wipro and Narayana Murthy of Infosys.

There are others like my friend's grandfather who did give and also taught his children to give 20 percent of their gross income to charity. He wanted them to physically give things to the poor. His children would go out to poor neighborhoods and distribute blankets and food in the winter to the homeless. The next day when they went back, they noticed that one person to whom they had given a blanket did not have it. They complained to their father that he had probably sold the blanket in exchange for a drink. The father said, give him another. He is needy.

In companies, we find some who bend over backward for their customers.

Companies I know will work with the community and with poorer people to help the community become more self-reliant and the poorer people more self-sufficient. They will offer executives for charitable work.

Zappos and Amazon are companies that are willing to give back to a customer who is unhappy, a replacement or its equivalent.

Truly customer-centric companies fall into this category.

Galbraith (2005)[1] describes customer centricity as a fundamental paradigm shift—away from the bias of the organization and its agents to operate on the side of the seller (i.e., itself) in any transaction, and toward operating "outside-in" on meeting the needs of the users or purchasers of its products or services. This approach to organizing people and work embeds many HR and OD best practices, including self-management, direct and frank communication, individual change agency, and team-based decision-making, and places these qualities firmly in the service of better outcomes for the end user, for business, and for employee engagement.

They fit into quadrant 1, top left of the chart that follows.

Mahajan Giving and Taking Matrix

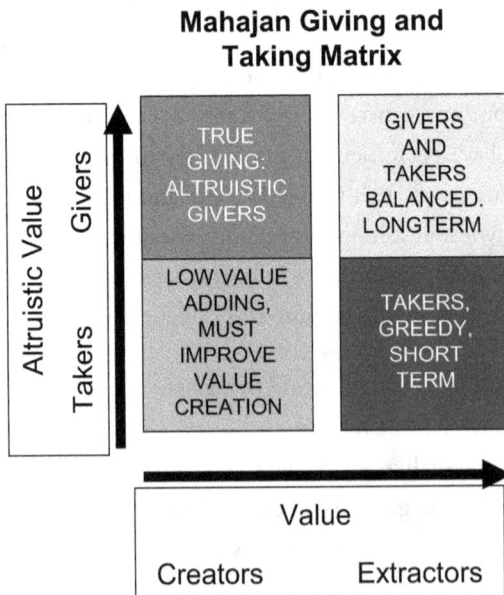

[1]J. R. Galbraith. 2005. *Designing the Customer-Centric Organization: A Guide to Strategy, Structure, and Process* (New York: Wiley).

2. Balanced, Long-Term Thinking: This category includes people who give to get (in a generous way, not in a mean fashion). Others are also generous givers if they see how it will help them or give them a return in the future. Many people fall into this category. Most companies are in this category and balance Value Creation and Value Extraction. Many business executives fit this mode, as do many workers.

The company I worked for, Continental Can, fell into this category in a nice, generous, caring way. Our account manager for a company knew most people in the company, including the CEO, the CXOs, and even the third-shift supervisor. He knew when someone was graduating or getting married and gave gifts. We all entertained lavishly. I myself entertained people some of whom I never met again. These people still remember the lunch or dinner with me because of the unexpected treat.

If one of our customers complained, we would have a team at his location to solve his problems, however small it was. In fact the customer would get embarrassed and tell the salesperson of the problem, asking him not to let me (the CEO) know. We also had customer services people who could run our material (or product) on his machines like a charm when his people had problems with it. Consequently, our product ran with the lowest spoilage compared with our competitors'.

Why do I put them in the second category? Because the giver would always get something in return. For example,

> ## Givers Vs. Takers
>
> ### Taker's Values
>
> - Wealth (money, material possessions)
> - Power (dominance, control over others)
> - Pleasure (enjoying life)
> - Winning (doing better than others)
>
> ### Giver's Values
>
> - Helpfulness (working for the well-being of others)
> - Responsibility (being dependable)
> - Social justice (caring for the disadvantaged)
> - Compassion (responding to the needs of others)
>
> https://economictimes.indiatimes.com/ givers-vs-takers-who-succeeds-in-an-organ- isation/articleshow/47628479.cms

they would know about changes in the client company before competition did and forestall any negative impact.

I had a boss at Continental who taught me the art of reverse negotiation. He taught me to give more to a vendor or an employee than he was expecting, thus getting his loyalty in return.

I remember I was negotiating polystyrene (PS) prices with a major supplier. The going rate was 31.5 cents per pound. I agreed to 32.5 cents a pound. My reasoning was that PS prices were going to double. It turned out that they went up to 67 cents a pound in 6 months. Our supplier held their prices with us for a much longer time than they did for our competitors, who had bought at 31.5 cents per pound, giving us a great cost advantage for a period of time.

Another example was when we were to buy a second machine from a supplier. It was a custom-made machine. The first machine was at a throwaway price because the supplier was desperate to sell to us. We also had a 10 percent penalty for late delivery. The machine was delivered late and we took the penalty. The supplier supported us magnificently, flying people out from Germany to help us when needed.

We got ready to buy the second machine, and I negotiated a good price. When I chatted with my boss, he asked me if I was happy with the supplier. I said very happy. He suggested I consider giving them the 10 percent penalty back. He asked, would it really make a difference to our cost of manufacture?. It really made a small difference and so I offered to give them the penalty money back. They were absolutely dazed by this. Even today, 30 years later they remember me as an unusual businessman! This is giving so that one gets loyalty in return.

Continental Can is an example of a company trying hard to avoid Customer Value Starvation, and succeeding most of the time.

You have had this experience, when an airline upgrades you free and unexpectedly, or does something really nice to you, like offering you the use of the lounge free.

3. The moment an Amazon reseller says give me a good rating before I change your purchase to a working one, we know that he wants a quid pro quo, and that puts him in the third category (lower left in chart).

People who do not give because they do not see what is in it for them. Many people are in this category. You will notice some companies that are in this category and pretend to be customer conscious but are really company centric. They are sometimes givers and sometimes takers.

Some companies also fall into this category. They are tough with customers. They will not take items back.

In India, if you buy a cell phone from a vendor, and it does not work, they will not replace it. They will ask you to take it to the repair shop of the supplier, such as Samsung or Apple. These people do not see what they will get by replacing the phone. They may lose a customer 2 years from now, but that is too far in the future.

They fall into the third category.

4. Takers or Extractors: Lastly, there those that pretend to help or give and do nothing. They just don't have it in them to give. They just take. Sometimes our very good friends fall into this category. They are friends till tested. Many companies that focus on Value Extraction are in this category.

   VW in its Dieselgate scandal, described in the previous chapter, falls into the fourth category.

Ask yourself which quadrant you fall into. Become givers and not just takers. Become a Value Creator and not a Value Starver.

I am sure you can think of many examples of people and companies. Ask a company call center or a telephone operator for the CEO's name. They will not give it, even though you can get it from the Internet. They just do not want to be helpful. These people lead to Value Starvation and Value Destruction.

That is why we are starting Creating Value centers, because we want more and more people to understand and contribute to creating value.

Adapted from an article by Gautam Mahajan

Are Firms Becoming More Human?

I have been wondering why firms pretend not to be human. I am writing this chapter to help companies and executives to create value and reduce Customer Value Starvation in the future. All of you need to think about this as you plan for the future.

First, one must accept that firms are really human, though they often pretend not to be. This is based on a simple thought: They are run and manned by people. This feeling within firms that they are inanimate is a major reason for the culture being nonhuman centric.

With digitization and automation, there is an upheaval now. Humans are being partly replaced by robots. AI is being used to answer day-to-day questions via chatbots. Workers on many mundane jobs are now being replaced by machines, so there will be fewer humans within the companies. Thus, companies will have a greater reason to pretend to be less human. This, of course, reduces Customer and Employee Value.

Customers, especially the younger ones, are comfortable with Internet-based interactions, including e-mails. Getting e-mails on your mobile a few years ago was a novelty. Today it is a necessity. The younger customers are getting used to nonhuman companies and nonhuman interaction. They are comfortable with robots, and working on the Internet/mobile.

One of the downsides of automation and AI is loss of jobs. What will these jobless people do? They need to be retrained to make them re-employable.

Those people left behind in companies that are reliant on automation and robots will need more service skills in an automated world. History has shown deep automation in industries like banking led to a crisis 20 years ago, because of job losses. Today, banks, for example, are making deep labor cuts in departments, including customer-facing people and back-end people. Those who are left have to be trained in new working ways and skills. Is this meant to add more value? For whom? The company or the customer? Guess who will lose?

Customers are expecting and getting used to more voice/data/Internet type of interaction and less face-to-face or direct interaction. This requires more humanness in the back-end machines. Services have to be more personalized, and help the customer manage his portfolio, his home, his transportation. The demand for services will increase and that for goods will decrease as demographics change to a larger aging population.

Care-giving services, like caring for old people, will need people, and in countries where population is decreasing this could be a problem. In companies, reduction of caring staff could lead to reduced customer value, though costs will reduce. Much better customer support will be needed with the people left after automation.

Will this reduce humanness, or reduce customer value? Well, there will have to be *creative destruction* of jobs because new skills will be needed with automation of routine processes and back-end work. Very well-designed customer support will be required. So, all of us looking into the future must pay heed to this.

A positive could be, for example, customized products, including mortgage products, all being given to the customer in 10 minutes with machine decision-making help. This will happen because AI will enable a deeper understanding of customers and make decision-making easier.

Humans will survive because there will still be a need for curiosity, creativity, and communication, and for using my 6As of awareness (and curiosity), ability, agility, anticipation, ambidextrousness, and attitude. And all this with listening empathy.

These skills do not exist and will have to be taught. And new jobs such as mixed reality experience designer, algorithm mechanic, and universal service adviser will emerge.

And so the inhuman companies (read bosses) have decided what their people have to do and what their customers should expect. Nowhere do they talk about themselves and their humanness.

The human touch requires deep emotional understanding. Retraining will have to include soft skills along with software and digital thinking. New AI and digitization aid humans to improve their soft skills by reminding them to be more thoughtful and empathetic in their customer interactions. Simultaneously, the training will be on improving technology skills of the people. The company's people will have to apply their humanness with sector knowledge, technical know-how, and human skills.

A BrightEdge survey states that 60 percent of the marketers that were surveyed say they will be using AI or automation. Thirty-one percent say this will improve customer understanding, 27 percent cite productivity gains, and only 8 percent claim higher ROI. The major prize is personalization.

Other questions:

Will the remaining workforce be more human, more caring?

Will added data collection allow better customer value to be created?

Will the bosses become more human so as to create customer value? Will companies become more human and accessible and less inanimate?

I can (and I am sure you can) give examples of companies not being helpful and showing their not so human face, leading to Customer Value Starvation. Let me give you examples of the inhuman face of companies.

I was in San Francisco and had to go to San Francisco General for emergency treatment. I had medical insurance, and the hospital billed the insurance company, which did not pay, as the policy would only reimburse payments made by me. I tried to pay the hospital, but they would only let me know how much I owed, but would not let me pay the bill. They would not give me relevant information on payment or give me bills the insurance company could use to reimburse me. I found it very difficult to communicate with the hospital. Try doing this from India.

Finally, I called Tata AIG in India and the call center put me in touch with someone who was willing to listen to me and go beyond the rules. They said they would waive the reimbursement rule and pay the hospital directly. They were human in understanding my predicament and created value for me.

A second example is a large group of doctors, where I went for follow-up treatment. The doctor and the staff treated me, my predicament of being unwell in a foreign country, and just helped me out in all kinds of different ways. They never worried about billing. They were always accessible and caring. I could call and get answers and see them without an appointment. They also gave me a care kit free of charge to help me on my journey back to India from San Francisco. Great customer value.

A great example is Air India during the floods in Mumbai (described earlier) a few years ago. The airport was closed for 2 days. Passengers with other airlines were stranded as their staff had left. Air India had its entire staff at the airport and took care of and fed passengers (even from other airlines). What caring!

Would this have happened if there was no human staff or reduced human staff (replaced by robots)?

I don't want to leave you with questions. I want to leave you with actions:

Accept you are human and your company is human.

Notice when the company pretends to be not human with employees, partners, and customers. How can you change this?

Does the company ask you to wear a not so human company cap and ask you to deal with others wearing that kind of a cap?

Ask how you can make the company more human.

Finally, ask how you can make your systems more human. Ask how you can design your AI and nonhuman assets to be more human.

See the difference it will make. Your customers and your people will notice this. You will leave the not so human companies and people behind. You will avoid Customer Value Starvation.

Ways to Create Customer Loyalty

It is so important that companies try their level best to create long-term customer loyalty. One step is to avoid Customer Value Starvation, which destroys every other positive measure companies take to create value.

This is a simple guideline for all levels of organizations:

1. Do Not Annoy (DNA) the customer.
2. Prevent Customer Value Starvation and achieve zero Customer Value Starvation complaints.
3. Have a good product.
4. Give excellent customer service and support. Avoid customer disservice.
5. Tell the customer how good you are and prove it.
6. Be employee focused.
7. Focus on the next time and make it better and memorable in a good way.

Read Moshe's "Mona Shaw" article also to see how loyalty is destroyed.

Can Customer Value Starvation Make Us Mona Shaws?

by Moshe Davidow

Moshe Davidow, Customer Service Expert, CEO of Service2Profit, and Professor at the Ono Academic Center.

There is no better way to end this book than to use Moshe's warning to companies.

In October 2007, Mona Shaw borrowed her husband's hammer and went to Comcast headquarters in Manassas, VA. She swung her hammer at monitors, computers, and telephones, yelling "Do I have your attention, now?" This was after a long period of time where Comcast had jerked her around. For her actions, she received a fine and a suspended sentence. She became an overnight sensation as *the* person who stood up to corporate bullying. She was even a guest of honor on a *Dr. Phil* episode on Vigilante Justice. Several articles were written about her exploits, including one where the author entreated companies to give their customers a hammer. His intention was clear. We need to give customers a safety valve where they can complain when the bureaucracy threatens to drive them away. Somebody who can step in and stop the carnage in its tracks; somebody to make sure the customer is not taken advantage of. This is value creation, at its best. We are clearly not there yet, 13 years later.

After yet another flight from hell on Delta Airlines 10 years ago, I sent in a complaint and was told there was nothing they would do. I sent a letter to the head of the complaint department, and then to the head of operations, and finally to the CEO. Each letter was responded to by the same person, who acknowledged that she was in charge of answering all corporate complaints, to keep a buffer between the customers and management. I have not flown Delta in 10 years.

The hotel that cares, Marriott, canceled all my miles 2 years ago, because I did not stay at their property for 2 years (there were reasons which Marriott made no attempt to learn). I complained that loyalty is supposed to be a two-way street. They have upheld their policy through all of my letters, pointing out that it was their discretion. I have not stayed at a Marriott since (despite five opportunities), and had my name taken off their mailing list.

Amazon, which claims to be customer centric, has done everything in its power to not answer my request for an explanation about a firm-centric change in their bookselling policy that has caused me to stop buying books from Amazon for the past 2 years. When I couldn't get a response by e-mail, I even sent a registered letter, which was never answered. In a chat with a representative, they denied the change had even taken place.

While looking for an article on the e-Gain website, I accessed their chat button, only to be told that they were only there for presale service. They sent me the e-mail of customer support. I sent them a letter asking about the article, and was answered that they would not answer the e-mail because I did not attach my customer account number. I answered that I don't have an account number because I am not a customer. They responded that they would not answer my e-mail since I did not include my customer account number.

These are all examples of Customer Value Starvation, and they all lead to the loss of a customer. In the first three cases, they all wanted me to come back. Why would I return to a company that does not value me as a customer? When bureaucracy becomes more important than the customer, then everybody loses.

According to the Customer Rage Studies in the United States, between 50 and 60 percent of all complainants say they got nothing in return from the company, and about 80 percent of the complainants were not completely satisfied with the company response. Guess what they are telling their friends about the slippery slope of value creation starvation?

In the back of my head, a small voice is asking, where is my hammer? If you build walls to keep customers away from management, we will look for hammers to break them down. Your Choice.

Moshe Davidow, Customer Service Expert, CEO of Service2Profit and Professor at the Ono Academic Center.

SECTION 5

Discussion and Conclusion

From a reading of the book, and the examples given, it becomes abundantly clear that the design and a pursuit of a new strategy, process, product, and service looks predominantly at the positive value creation for the company or for the people in control. Most do not pay heed to the value destruction potential, especially on customers and other stakeholders. They even ignore this, or in their minds, minimize its impact. Much of this primarily impacts third parties such as citizens, customers, employees (loss of jobs), and society.

However, from a corporate viewpoint, potential value destruction studies and analysis during the design process could have revealed better design, better processes, more effective service, and more pervasive products. This includes risk analysis, compliance studies, operational analysis, environmental and societal thinking. Not doing so can result in a loss to the corporate entity. Companies can benefit themselves and their stakeholders, including society, from such analysis before the fact, rather than suffering after the fact or causing value destruction (or value starvation) for people and society and for the company itself.

The aim of companies should be to increase Customer Value. The starting point is avoiding Customer Value Starvation.

In conclusion, this opens up the possibility of better value-creating strategies. This means a different way of thinking, and a more reasoned solution. This has to be taught and embraced by practitioners. This becomes a fertile area of research for companies and academics to analyze value destruction potential to create more value. We must get away from reactive and *after the fact* analysis to proactive value creation and reducing value destruction, and learning from value destruction potential.

Ideas to Prevent Value Starvation

The customer experience thinking has put the pursuit of delight ahead of the pursuit of ending misery. This thinking also emanates from the thinking that hunting is more prestigious than farming. Taking care of customers is secondary to getting new customers.

The real customer misery experience comes when companies believe that they can throw their responsibilities onto the customer.

The best product is one we are satisfied with and which gives us a good experience. We expect the product to work and that it will meet our needs. If it does, we are happy.

Companies must take responsibility for a new product that turns out to be faulty during its first use, and not expect the customer to be responsible for taking care of it through middle persons. Thus, a faulty new phone is the responsibility of the manufacturer and should be handled as such.

In use and in service, companies must remember if the product does not work or has to go through an update, downtime must be minimised. There is no point in the middle of summer to say the air conditioner will be repaired in 3 weeks' time.

In all cases, companies must be aware of and prevent Customer Value Starvation and not promote it by neglect, by turning the responsibility to someone else (especially not the customer). Companies should avoid the myriad value starvation procedures that end up in not getting to someone to talk to, complain to and to hold their hands, and worse still being ignored. They should feel they are being treated as customers and not just a "sale"!

Some ideas not discussed earlier in detail:

- Companies do not realize the serious cost to them and the customer of Value Starvation. The time and effort on either side is enormous. This should be examined. Once a realization sets in that Customer Value Starvation is an area of cost reduction and also engenders customer retention, then companies will take it seriously.
- The company must imbibe a Do Not Annoy (DNA) culture.
- Zero Customer Value Starvation complaints are possible because such complaints are a result of the company's ignorance or not noticing or not caring. They are easily avoidable.
- Companies must put Customer Value and Customer Value Starvation in their vocabulary. When they examine the Customer Journey,

they should examine the Value Starvation. Companies should look for points where starvation could happen and is happening. They should also look at complaints that fall into Customer Value Starvation (and remember that for every one complaint there are 10 other people who do not complain), and then ensure there is a systemic improvement to prevent this from happening with others.

- While looking at some areas relevant to the customer, like Customer Journey, Customer Experience, Value Proposition (price justification), do not fail to look at Customer Value and Customer Value Starvation. Learn how to identify, measure, and improve these.

- In their customer strategy session, Customer Value Starvation should become an important area of inspection, introspection, and debate for companies.

- Companies should incorporate Customer Circles, described in Gautam's book *Total Customer Value Management[1]*, to help employees figure out what causes Customer Value Starvation and with management find ways to prevent this for the short and long term.

- Schools and colleges should look at adding a discussion on value creation in their courses, start courses on value creation, or even a value school, such as the one the University of Kobe has in Japan, or creating value centers, such as the one at the University of Maryland, and the one coming up at the University of Aalborg in Denmark. A Creating Value School is coming up at the Japan Advanced Institute of Science and Technology.

- Customer Value Starvation is also a defect in our system. These defects must be removed. The time has come for zero defects and zero complaints. Why are these complaints occurring? How do we prevent them (for example, repackaged returned goods from being sent out by a company's reseller; common complaints like I cannot hear well on my brand new phone because no one suggested removing the plastic protector before use)? Why are companies happy about killing customers? Don't they see that the death of customers will also kill them?

---

[1]Total Customer Value Management: Transforming Business Thinking, Sage Response Books, 2011

- Create value for the customer. Do not starve the customer of value by putting your convenience above the customer's convenience. Also put the customer's concerns ahead of yours!

Perhaps the most important thing for companies to understand is the 6As (Awareness, Attitude, Ability, Agility, Anticipation, and Ambidextrousness). The company and its employees should adopt these more diligently.

Awareness is probably the most important need for an executive when thinking of or looking at customers. To become aware, employees must have self-esteem, also something the company should build. Practicing the 6As will reduce cases of Customer Value Starvation!

We prefer Customer Circles, described in my book *Total Customer Value Management*, over training. Training is for dogs; education is for humans. The Customer Circles have worked well around the world.

Lastly, humanize your business. This will happen when you are proactive and anticipatory. Proactive means you are aware, you notice, and you react. You should be doing things before the customer asks you to. Think how you can give peace of mind to the customer. Be willing to relax rigid rules if the situation warrants it. Then you avoid Customer Value Starvation and are on the path to Value Creation.

Remember, Walmart founder Sam Walton once said, "There is only one boss. The customer. And he can fire everybody in the company from the chairman on down, simply by spending his money somewhere else."

Appendix

CEOs Who Signed Off on the New Purpose of a Company in August 2019, Business Roundtable

CEOs who signed off on the New Purpose of a Company to create Value for all and hopefully avoid Customer Value Starvation:

- Kevin J. Wheeler, PRESIDENT AND CEO, A.O. SMITH CORPORATION
- Miles D. White, CHAIRMAN AND CEO, ABBOTT
- Julie Sweet, CEO DESIGNATE, ACCENTURE
- Carlos Rodriguez, PRESIDENT AND CEO, ADP
- Mike Burke, CHAIRMAN AND CEO, AECOM
- Andrés Gluski, PRESIDENT AND CEO, THE AES CORPORATION
- Daniel P. Amos, CHAIRMAN AND CEO, AFLAC
- Roger K. Newport, CEO, AK STEEL CORPORATION
- Brent Saunders, CHAIRMAN AND CEO, ALLERGAN PLC
- John O. Larsen, CHAIRMAN, PRESIDENT AND CEO, ALLIANT ENERGY
- Lee Styslinger, III, CHAIRMAN AND CEO, ALTEC, INC.
- Jeffrey P. Bezos, FOUNDER AND CEO, AMAZON
- Doug Parker, CHAIRMAN AND CEO, AMERICAN AIRLINES
- Nicholas K. Akins, CHAIRMAN, PRESIDENT AND CEO, AMERICAN ELECTRIC POWER
- Stephen J. Squeri, CHAIRMAN AND CEO, AMERICAN EXPRESS

- James D. Taiclet, CHAIRMAN, PRESIDENT AND CEO, AMERICAN TOWER CORPORATION
- James Cracchiolo, CHAIRMAN AND CEO, AMERIPRISE FINANCIAL
- Gail Koziara Boudreaux, PRESIDENT AND CEO, ANTHEM, INC.
- Greg Case, CEO, AON
- Tim Cook, CEO, APPLE
- Eric Foss, CHAIRMAN, PRESIDENT AND CEO, ARAMARK
- Alan B. Colberg, PRESIDENT AND CEO, ASSURANT
- Randall Stephenson, CHAIRMAN AND CEO, AT&T INC.
- John A. Hayes, CHAIRMAN, PRESIDENT AND CEO, BALL CORPORATION
- Brian Moynihan, CHAIRMAN OF THE BOARD AND CEO, BANK OF AMERICA
- José (Joe) E. Almeida, CHAIRMAN, PRESIDENT AND CEO, BAXTER INTERNATIONAL INC.
- Philip Blake, PRESIDENT, BAYER USA
- Joe Davis, MD AND SENIOR PARTNER; CHAIRMAN North America, BCG
- Brendan P. Bechtel, CHAIRMAN AND CEO, BECHTEL GROUP, INC.
- Corie Barry, CEO, BEST BUY CO., INC.
- Laurence D. Fink, CHAIRMAN AND CEO, BLACKROCK, INC.
- Charles W. Scharf, CHAIRMAN AND CEO, BNY MELLON
- Dennis A. Muilenburg, CHAIRMAN, PRESIDENT AND CEO, THE BOEING COMPANY
- Frédéric B. Lissalde, PRESIDENT AND CEO, BORGWARNER INC.
- Robert Dudley, GROUP CEO, BP PLC
- Giovanni Caforio, CHAIRMAN AND CEO, BRISTOL-MYERS SQUIBB
- Maurice R. Greenberg, CHAIRMAN AND CEO, C.V. STARR AND CO., INC.
- Kewsong Lee, CO-CEO, THE CARLYLE GROUP

- D. James Umpleby III, CHAIRMAN AND CEO, CATERPILLAR, INC.
- Robert E. Sulentic, PRESIDENT AND CEO, CBRE GROUP, INC.
- W. Anthony Will, PRESIDENT AND CEO, CF INDUSTRIES
- Michael K. Wirth, CHAIRMAN AND CEO, CHEVRON CORPORATION
- Evan G. Greenberg, CHAIRMAN AND CEO, CHUBB
- David M. Cordani, PRESIDENT AND CEO, CIGNA
- Chuck Robbins, CHAIRMAN AND CEO, CISCO SYSTEMS, INC.
- Michael L. Corbat, CEO, CITIGROUP, INC.
- Hubertus M. Mühlhäuser, CEO, CNH INDUSTRIAL
- James Quincey, CHAIRMAN AND CEO, THE COCA-COLA COMPANY
- Brian Humphries, CEO, COGNIZANT
- Brian L. Roberts, CHAIRMAN AND CEO, COMCAST CORPORATION
- Ryan M. Lance, CHAIRMAN AND CEO, CONOCOPHILLIPS COMPANY
- Wendell P. Weeks, CHAIRMAN, CEO, AND PRESIDENT, CORNING INCORPORATED
- Tom Linebarger, CHAIRMAN AND CEO, CUMMINS INC.
- Larry Merlo, PRESIDENT AND CEO, Customer Value Starvation HEALTH
- Hal Yoh, CHAIRMAN AND CEO, DAY AND ZIMMERMANN
- Michael S. Dell, CHAIRMAN AND CEO, DELL TECHNOLOGIES
- Punit Renjen, CEO, DELOITTE
- Jim Fitterling, CEO, DOW
- Lynn Good, CHAIRMAN, PRESIDENT AND CEO, DUKE ENERGY
- JM Lawrie, CHAIRMAN, PRESIDENT AND CEO, DXC TECHNOLOGY
- Mark J. Costa, CHAIRMAN AND CEO, EASTMAN CHEMICAL COMPANY
- Craig Arnold, CHAIRMAN AND CEO, EATON

- Pedro J. Pizarro, PRESIDENT AND CEO, EDISON INTERNATIONAL
- Darren W. Woods, CHAIRMAN AND CEO, EXXON MOBIL CORPORATION
- Carmine Di Sibio, GLOBAL CHAIRMAN AND CEO, EY
- Frederick W. Smith, CHAIRMAN AND CEO, FEDEX CORPORATION
- Gary Norcross, CHAIRMAN, PRESIDENT AND CEO, FIS
- Revathi Advaithi, CEO, FLEX
- Carlos M. Hernandez, CEO, FLUOR CORPORATION
- James P. Hackett, PRESIDENT AND CEO, FORD MOTOR COMPANY
- Lachlan K. Murdoch, EXECUTIVE CHAIRMAN AND CEO, FOX CORPORATION
- Richard C. Adkerson, VICE CHAIRMAN, PRESIDENT AND CEO, FREEPORT-MCMORAN INC.
- Phebe Novakovic, CHAIRMAN AND CEO, GENERAL DYNAMICS CORPORATION
- Mary Barra, CHAIRMAN AND CEO, GENERAL MOTORS COMPANY
- David M. Solomon, CHAIRMAN AND CEO, THE GOLDMAN SACHS GROUP, INC.
- Deanna M. Mulligan, PRESIDENT AND CEO, GUARDIAN LIFE INSURANCE COMPANY OF AMERICA
- Gerald W. Evans, CEO, HANESBRANDS INC.
- Dinesh C. Paliwal, PRESIDENT AND CEO, HARMAN INTERNATIONAL
- Steven R. Swartz, PRESIDENT AND CEO, HEARST CORPORATION
- Craig Menear, CHAIRMAN, CEO AND PRESIDENT, THE HOME DEPOT
- Darius Adamczyk, CHAIRMAN AND CEO, HONEYWELL
- Mike Petters, PRESIDENT AND CEO, HUNTINGTON INGALLS INDUSTRIES
- Ginni Rometty, CHAIRMAN, PRESIDENT AND CEO, IBM CORPORATION
- Charles Phillips, CEO, INFOR

- Mark S. Sutton, CHAIRMAN AND CEO, INTERNATIONAL PAPER CO.
- Michael I. Roth, CHAIRMAN AND CEO, INTERPUBLIC GROUP
- Linda H. Apsey, PRESIDENT AND CEO, ITC HOLDINGS CORP.
- Steve Demetriou, CHAIR AND CEO, JACOBS
- Samuel R. Allen, CHAIRMAN AND CEO, JOHN DEERE
- Alex Gorsky, CHAIRMAN OF THE BOARD AND CEO, JOHNSON AND JOHNSON
- George R. Oliver, CHAIRMAN AND CEO, JOHNSON CONTROLS
- Jamie Dimon, CHAIRMAN AND CEO, JPMORGAN CHASE AND CO.
- Beth E. Mooney, CHAIRMAN AND CEO, KEYCORP
- Bruce E. Grewcock, CEO AND CHAIRMAN OF THE BOARD, KIEWIT CORPORATION
- Lynne M. Doughtie, CHAIRMAN AND CEO, KPMG LLP
- William M. Brown, CHAIRMAN AND CEO, L3HARRIS TECHNOLOGIES, INC.
- Beth E. Ford, PRESIDENT AND CEO, LAND O'LAKES, INC.
- Roger A. Krone, CHAIRMAN AND CEO, LEIDOS
- Stuart Miller, EXECUTIVE CHAIRMAN, LENNAR CORPORATION
- Marillyn A. Hewson, CHAIRMAN, PRESIDENT AND CEO, LOCKHEED MARTIN CORPORATION
- Bhavesh V. (Bob) Patel, CEO, LYONDELLBASELL INDUSTRIES
- Jeff Gennette, CHAIRMAN AND CEO, MACY'S, INC.
- Mark Trudeau, PRESIDENT AND CEO, MALLINCKRODT PHARMACEUTICALS
- Lee M. Tillman, CHAIRMAN, PRESIDENT AND CEO, MARATHON OIL CORPORATION
- Gary R. Heminger, CHAIRMAN AND CEO, MARATHON PETROLEUM CORPORATION
- Arne M. Sorenson, PRESIDENT AND CEO, MARRIOTT INTERNATIONAL, INC.

- Roger W. Crandall, CHAIRMAN, PRESIDENT AND CEO, MASSMUTUAL
- Ajay Banga, PRESIDENT AND CEO, MASTERCARD
- Lawrence E. Kurzius, CHAIRMAN, PRESIDENT AND CEO, MCCORMICK AND COMPANY, INC.
- Brian Tyler, CEO, MCKESSON CORPORATION
- Omar Ishrak, CHAIRMAN AND CEO, MEDTRONIC PLC
- Michel Khalaf, PRESIDENT AND CEO, METLIFE
- Sanjay Mehrotra, PRESIDENT AND CEO, MICRON TECHNOLOGY
- Ken Moelis, CHAIRMAN AND CEO, MOELIS AND COMPANY
- James P. Gorman, CHAIRMAN AND CEO, MORGAN STANLEY
- Greg Brown, CHAIRMAN AND CEO, MOTOROLA SOLUTIONS
- Adena T. Friedman, PRESIDENT AND CEO, NASDAQ
- Thomas C. Nelson, CHAIRMAN, PRESIDENT AND CEO, NATIONAL GYPSUM COMPANY
- Ted Mathas, CHAIRMAN, PRESIDENT AND CEO, NEW YORK LIFE INSURANCE CO.
- David L. Stover, CHAIRMAN AND CEO, NOBLE ENERGY, INC.
- Kathy Warden, CHAIRMAN, CEO AND PRESIDENT, NORTHROP GRUMMAN CORPORATION
- Steve Fisher, PRESIDENT AND CEO, NOVELIS
- Mauricio Gutierrez, PRESIDENT AND CEO, NRG ENERGY, INC.
- Safra Catz, CEO, ORACLE
- Brian Chambers, PRESIDENT AND CEO, OWENS CORNING
- Ramon Laguarta, CEO, PEPSICO
- Dr. Albert Bourla, CEO, PFIZER INC.
- Greg C. Garland, CHAIRMAN AND CEO, PHILLIPS 66
- Marc B. Lautenbach, PRESIDENT AND CEO, PITNEY BOWES
- Daniel J. Houston, CHAIRMAN, PRESIDENT AND CEO, PRINCIPAL
- David S. Taylor, CHAIRMAN OF THE BOARD, PRESIDENT AND CEO, THE PROCTER AND GAMBLE COMPANY

- Tricia Griffith, PRESIDENT AND CEO, PROGRESSIVE CORPORATION
- Bob Moritz, CHAIRMAN, PWC
- Steve Mollenkopf, CEO, QUALCOMM INCORPORATED
- Earl C. Austin, Jr., PRESIDENT AND CEO, QUANTA SERVICES
- Thomas A. Kennedy, CHAIRMAN AND CEO, RAYTHEON COMPANY
- Blake D. Moret, CHAIRMAN AND CEO, ROCKWELL AUTOMATION
- Douglas L. Peterson, PRESIDENT AND CEO, S&P GLOBAL
- Keith Block, CO-CEO, SALESFORCE
- Bill McDermott, CEO, SAP
- Jim Goodnight, CEO, SAS INSTITUTE
- Tamara L. Lundgren, PRESIDENT AND CEO, SCHNITZER STEEL INDUSTRIES, INC.
- Jeffrey W. Martin, CHAIRMAN AND CEO, SEMPRA ENERGY
- Lisa Davis, CEO, SIEMENS CORPORATION USA
- Egon Durban, MANAGING PARTNER AND MANAGING DIRECTOR, SILVER LAKE
- Thomas A. Fanning, CHAIRMAN, PRESIDENT AND CEO, SOUTHERN COMPANY
- James M. Loree, PRESIDENT AND CEO, STANLEY BLACK AND DECKER
- James P. Keane, PRESIDENT AND CEO, STEELCASE INC.
- Kevin Lobo, CHAIRMAN AND CEO, STRYKER
- John F. Fish, CHAIRMAN AND CEO, SUFFOLK
- Brian Cornell, CHAIRMAN AND CEO, TARGET
- Russell K. Girling, PRESIDENT AND CEO, TC ENERGY
- LeRoy T. Carlson, Jr., CEO, TELEPHONE AND DATA SYSTEMS, INC.
- Richard K. Templeton, CHAIRMAN, PRESIDENT AND CEO, TEXAS INSTRUMENTS INCORPORATED
- Rob Speyer, PRESIDENT AND CEO, TISHMAN SPEYER
- Alan D. Schnitzer, CHAIRMAN AND CEO, THE TRAVELERS COMPANIES INC.
- M. Troy Woods, CHAIRMAN, PRESIDENT AND CEO, TSYS

- Peter J. Davoren, PRESIDENT AND CEO, TURNER CONSTRUCTION CO.
- Lance M. Fritz, CHAIRMAN, PRESIDENT AND CEO, UNION PACIFIC
- Oscar Munoz, CEO, UNITED AIRLINES
- Gregory J. Hayes, CHAIRMAN AND CEO, UNITED TECHNOLOGIES CORPORATION
- David Abney, CHAIRMAN AND CEO, UPS
- Stuart Parker, CEO, USAA
- Mortimer J. Buckley, PRESIDENT AND CEO, VANGUARD
- Scott G. Stephenson, CHAIRMAN, PRESIDENT AND CEO, VERISK ANALYTICS
- Alfred F. Kelly Jr., CHAIRMAN AND CEO, VISA INC.
- Robert F. Smith, FOUNDER, CHAIRMAN AND CEO, VISTA EQUITY PARTNERS
- Curt Morgan, PRESIDENT AND CEO, VISTRA ENERGY
- Stefano Pessina, EXECUTIVE VICE CHAIRMAN AND CEO, WALGREENS BOOTS ALLIANCE
- Doug McMillon, PRESIDENT AND CEO, WALMART, INC.
- John J. Engel, CHAIRMAN, PRESIDENT AND CEO, WESCO INTERNATIONAL, INC.
- John F. Barrett, CHAIRMAN, PRESIDENT AND CEO, WESTERN AND SOUTHERN FINANCIAL GROUP
- Hikmet Ersek, CEO, WESTERN UNION
- Marc Bitzer, CHAIRMAN AND CEO, WHIRLPOOL CORPORATION
- Abidali Z. Neemuchwala, CEO AND MANAGING DIRECTOR, WIPRO LIMITED
- Michael J. Kasbar, CHAIRMAN, PRESIDENT AND CEO, WORLD FUEL SERVICES CORPORATION
- Jim Kavanaugh, CEO, WORLD WIDE TECHNOLOGY
- John Visentin, VICE CHAIRMAN AND CEO, XEROX CORPORATION
- Patrick Decker, PRESIDENT AND CEO, XYLEM INC.
- Anders Gustafsson, CEO, ZEBRA TECHNOLOGIES CORPORATION
- Michael Roman, CHAIRMAN OF THE BOARD AND CEO, 3M

About the Authors

Walter Vieira pioneered marketing consultancy in India, when he started Marketing Advisory Services, India, in 1975. Before that, he spent 14 years as a corporate executive with leading MNCs in the pharmaceutical industry.

As a consultant for 45 years, he has worked for MNCs, large Indian conglomerates, medium-sized businesses, central and state governments, and the social sector. He has worked across continents—from North America and Europe to Africa and Asia.

He has been a part-time journalist, has published over a thousand articles, and wrote the longest running column on management in *Business World*.

He has been Visiting Professor of Marketing at U.S. and Indian business schools, for example, Kellogg, Cornell, Lake Forest, Rady, NYU, Drexel, Bajaj Institute, and Administrative Staff College.

Walter has addressed World Conferences of Management Consultants in Rome, Yokohama, and Berlin and World Marketing Summits in Bangladesh, Tokyo, and New Delhi.

He was elected President of the Institute of Management Consultants of India, was Founder Chairman of the Asia Pacific Conference of Management Consultants, and was elected Chairman of the 45-country International Council of Management Consulting Institutes. Walter was awarded the Lifetime Achievement Award for Management Consulting in 2005, and the Lifetime Achievement Award for Marketing in 2009.

Walter has written the following books over a 40-year period:

- *Marketing: Key to Business Success Today* (with Professor C. Northcote Parkinson)
- *Marketing Is Business*
- *The Professional Salesman*
- *The New Sales Manager*
- *The Impatient Manager*

- *Succeed at Interviews*
- *The Winning Manager*
- *Manager to CEO*
- *Succeed at Examinations*
- *Retirement: Plan Now for Your Best Years* (with Professor C. Northcote Parkinson)
- *Marketing in a Digital and Data World* (with Brian Almeida)
- *5 Gs of Family Business* (with Professor Mita Dixit)
- *Entrepreneur: You Can Move Mountains*
- *World Passport for Global Managers*
- *Marketing Insights*

E-mail: waltervieira@gmail.com
Website: www.waltervieira.com

Gautam Mahajan, President of Customer Value Foundation, is the global thought leader in Customer Value and Value Creation. He mentors the Creating Value Alliance (creatingvalue.co) and is Editor of the *Journal of Creating Value* (jcv.sagepub.com). He is helping value creation centers in Denmark and at the University of Maryland, and the Value School at the University of Kobe, and the Creating Value School at the Japan Advanced Institute of Science and Technology in Japan. He is also an inventor with products being used around the world, and has 18 U.S. patents.

Gautam ran businesses for a Fortune 50 company in the United States for 17 years and has developed leaders, CEOs, and executives; consulted for Alcoa, DuPont, Continental Can, Reynolds, GE, GTE, ITC, Sealed Air, Azelis, Tata, Birla, Godrej, ITC, Toyo-Seikan, Viag, and Solvay. He is the author of six books: *Customer Value Investment, Value Dominant Logic, The Value Imperative, Total Customer Value Management, How Creating Customer Value Can Make You a Great Executive, and Value Creation*.

He was President of the Indo-American Chamber of Commerce and was Chairman, PlastIndia Committee; Vice President, All India Plastics Manufacturers Association; Trustee, Plastics Institute of America. He was a member of the U.S. India Think Tank. He was Chairman of the U.S. India Economics Relations Forum. Among his honors is a Fellowship from Harvard Business School and Illinois Institute of Technology. He was honored by the Illinois Institute of Technology with its Distinguished

Alumni award in 2001. Recently, he spoke at the Center for American and International Law in Dallas to an audience of 35 countries on India, and at Berlin in 2006 at the European Fine Chemicals Conference and in 2011 in New York, Akron, Columbus, Denver, Chicago, and California. He spoke to CEOs from 26 European companies in 2008. More recently, he conducted a workshop in Orlando (2012), Kuala Lumpur, San Diego, Vancouver and chaired an IQPC Telecom conference in Munich. He spoke at Singapore, Amsterdam (PPS), and Breda in December 2015 on creating value and getting a price for it. Other pricing conferences he spoke at are PPS in Orlando, Amsterdam, Bangkok, Berlin, Mumbai, and Delhi. He was written up in the *Wall Street Journal.* He also gave the first Distinguished Engineering lecture at Illinois followed by a Distinguished Management lecture. In September 2011, he spent time in the United States talking about Indo-U.S. relations and how to improve them. He has given lectures to bankers at the RBI College of Agri Banking. Recent talks have been in San Francisco, Dallas, Austin, London, Berlin (where he chaired a pricing conference and was a keynote), New York, Boston, Leicester, and Kobe. He has lectured at IITs at Madras, Jammu, Mandi, Delhi, and Gandhinagar and abroad to faculty, staff, and students in the United States and Europe.

Mr. Mahajan is a graduate of IIT Madras, where he was an Institute Merit Scholar, has a master's degree in mechanics and has completed his PhD coursework from the Illinois Institute of Technology and an MBA from Suffolk University.

E-mail: Gautam.Mahajan@gmail.com
Website: CustomerValueFoundation.com

Index

OTHER TITLES IN OUR SERVICE SYSTEMS AND INNOVATIONS IN BUSINESS AND SOCIETY COLLECTION

Jim Spohrer and Haluk Demirkan, *Editors*

- *The Value Imperative* by Gautam Mahajan
- *Co-Design, Volume I: Practical Ideas for Learning Across Complex Systems* by Mark Gaten and Stefan Cantore
- *Co-Design, Volume II: Practical Ideas for Designing Across Complex Systems* by Mark Gatenby
- *Co-Design, Volume III: Practical Ideas for Developing Across Complex Systems* by Stefan Cantore
- *Service Excellence in Organizations, Volume I: Eight Key Steps to Follow and Achieve It* by Fiona Urquhart
- *Service Excellence in Organizations, Volume II: Eight Key Steps to Follow and Achieve It* by Fiona Urquhart
- *Obtaining Value from Big Data for Service Systems, Volume I: Big Data Management* by Stephen H. Kaisler and Frank Armour
- *Obtaining Value from Big Data for Service Systems, Volume II: Big Data Technology* by Stephen H. Kaisler and Frank Armour
- *Everything Old is New Again: How Entrepreneurs Use Discourse Themes to Reclaim Abandoned Urban Spaces* by Miriam Plavin-Masterman
- *How Creating Customer Value Makes You a Great Executive* by Gautam Mahajan
- *Sustainability and the City: The Service Approach* by Adi Wolfson
- *The Accelerating TechnOnomic Medium ('ATOM'): It's Time to Upgrade the Economy* by Kartik Gada
- *How Can Digital Technologies Improve Public Services and Governance?* by Nagy K. Hanna
- *Collaborative Innovation: How Clients and Service Providers Can Work By Design to Achieve It* by Tony Morgan

Concise and Applied Business Books

The Collection listed above is one of 30 business subject collections that Business Expert Press has grown to make BEP a premiere publisher of print and digital books. Our concise and applied books are for...

- Professionals and Practitioners
- Faculty who adopt our books for courses
- Librarians who know that BEP's Digital Libraries are a unique way to offer students ebooks to download, not restricted with any digital rights management
- Executive Training Course Leaders
- Business Seminar Organizers

Business Expert Press books are for anyone who needs to dig deeper on business ideas, goals, and solutions to everyday problems. Whether one print book, one ebook, or buying a digital library of 110 ebooks, we remain the affordable and smart way to be business smart. For more information, please visit **www.businessexpertpress.com**, or contact **sales@businessexpertpress.com**.

www.ingramcontent.com/pod-product-compliance
Lightning Source LLC
Chambersburg PA
CBHW061213220326
41599CB00025B/4627